T0247356

Little Books on Liturgy

Samuel Torvend, series editor

Also in the series:

Abide in Peace: Healing and Reconciliation by Marcus George
    Halley

For the Life of the World: The Essentials of Episcopal Worship by
    Samuel Torvend

GAIL RAMSHAW

MUCH FINE GOLD

THE REVISED COMMON LECTIONARY

A little book on liturgy

CHURCH
PUBLISHING
INCORPORATED

Unless otherwise noted, the Scripture quotations contained herein are from the New Revised Standard Version Bible, copyright © 1989 by the Division of Christian Education of the National Council of Churches of Christ in the United States of America. Used by permission. All rights reserved worldwide.

Church Publishing Incorporated
19 East 34th Street
New York, NY 10016

Cover design by Jennifer Kopec, 2Pug Design
Typeset by Progressive Publishing Services

Library of Congress Cataloging-in-Publication Data
A record of this book is available from the Library of Congress.

ISBN-13: 978-1-64065-422-8 (paperback)
ISBN-13: 978-1-64065-423-5 (ebook)

Contents

Introducing our Revised Common Lectionary

The decrees of the LORD are sure, making wise the simple.
More to be desired are they than gold, even much fine gold.
Psalm 19:7, 10

Praising the Word of God

Christians agree with Jews and Muslims that God speaks to believers, in the past and the present, in many different ways. We may hear these words from God in the sounds of the earth itself, in an interior voice inside us, in the speech of a friend or a stranger, in music and art, and in various religious rituals. But Christians hear the Word of God most definitively in the Bible, especially in the scripture as it is proclaimed in the worshiping assembly. It is this proclaimed word of God that this small book addresses.

Among the biblical texts that have prominent place in Christian worship are the poems that are called psalms. The psalms, honored by the Church as the Word of God, are filled with praise for the Word of God. For the believer, to read and to receive the empowering religious literature that fills the Bible is to open up the self to God. Psalm 119 offers compelling comparisons to describe this transformational word: the Law is better than thousands of silver pieces (v. 72), sweeter than honey (v. 103), a lamp to my feet and a light to my path (v. 105), my heritage forever (v. 111), and like great spoil (v. 162).[1] "Truly I love your commandments more than gold, more than fine gold" (v. 127). In Psalm 19, the author employs synonyms to name this word: the Law, the testimony of LORD, God's statutes, God's commandment, the judgments of the LORD—these are more to be desired than gold. Other biblical translations of Psalm 19 call this Word God's instructions, decrees, precepts, and ordinances. But all translations agree that the Word of God is more to be desired than gold, more than "much fine gold" (v. 10).

Each week worshipers listen to short selections chosen from the Bible, acclaiming what we hear as "the Word of the Lord," "what the Spirit is saying to God's people." Our lectionary invites us to join with many Christians to support these readings by singing and praying those psalms that praise "the Word of the Lord" as sweeter than honey, as a light to my path. At the annual Easter Vigil, after we receive the word from Baruch or Proverbs that speaks of divine Wisdom, we join in Psalm 19 to sing of this fine gold. On a Sunday in Lent, after receiving the commandments as delivered on Mount Sinai, we laud this teaching as if it were fine gold. In September when we hear that the spirit of Moses was shared with seventy elders, we once again rely on Psalm 19 to describe their prophesies as more than gold. With the words of Psalm 19, we praise the word heard through the lectionary, to laud what the Spirit is saying, as more to be desired than much fine gold.

---

1. All biblical quotations in this book come from the *New Revised Standard Version* of the Bible.

Learning Our Lectionary

The term "lectionary" is used to designate the list of readings appointed for proclamation during assembly worship, as well as for the bound book in which the readings are printed sequentially. In this little book we will study the list of readings that is titled the Revised Common Lectionary.[2] The Revised Common Lectionary is appointed for use in the Episcopal Church and is recommended or adopted by many churches worldwide. It is hoped that the more we know about these readings and why they have been selected for Sundays and feasts, the more meaningful our praise will be in recognizing that this Word of God is better than gold.

First in chapter 1 we ask: what is the design of the lectionary? What is the logic of the ordering of readings throughout the year? Then we investigate why this lectionary serves the Church as well as it does. How does this lectionary enrich our worship, enhance our daily devotion, and shine through us to share God's radiance with others? Four descriptors will guide our discussion: examining the lectionary as ecumenical (chapter 2), metaphoric (chapter 3), historic (chapter 4), and contemporary (chapter 5) assists us in valuing this set of readings as more desirable than much fine gold. The final chapter addresses yet other issues.

---

2. See Consultation on Common Texts, *The Revised Common Lectionary,* 20th Anniversary Annotated Edition (Minneapolis: Fortress Press, 2012). Alternatively, *The Revised Common Lectionary: Years A, B, C, and Holy Days according to the use of The Episcopal Church* (New York: Church Publishing, 2007).

You might preface your study of our lectionary by imagining how you might design a worthy lectionary. Should a lectionary cite from every book of the Bible, or should it focus on only the central parts of the scripture? Should the citations be easily grasped? Is it better to have several short readings or one long one? Should the lectionary include or omit troubling passages? Should the lectionary assume that the hearers have some knowledge of basic Christian vocabulary, or should it be entirely available also to seekers? Will it matter which biblical translation is used? Should an entire Church body use the same lectionary?

The hope is that the more we understand the plan and potential of this lectionary, the more we will appreciate its proclamation. This small book will encourage us to learn something about the original biblical location from which the readings are taken and to understand the specific seasonal intentions of the selections. Why were these texts appointed for this Sunday, and where are they headed? We may become more inspired to prepare for assembly worship by reading through the selections beforehand. We will come to expect that the hymns we sing; the preaching we hear; the colors, music, and art that adorn our worship space; the catechesis that our parish offers to children and adults; and our home worship between Sundays will support the lectionary.

Becoming "lectionary Christians" is one style of Christian spirituality, and those who live by the lectionary heartily recommend it. May this study and your conversation concerning it entice you to become a lectionary Christian, affirming the Church's lectionary, not with vexation, but with enthusiasm and joy.

At the outset, we explore the following questions:

1. Psalm 19 is a poem. Do you ever choose to read poetry? What kind? If not, why not?

2. Describe some behavior pattern or ritual that you have gladly adopted, having been convinced of its value. When and why did you begin this practice?

3. What is some discipline that is forced upon you that you resent? Why do you resent it?

4. What is your experience of a church that uses a lectionary? Do you judge that experience to be spiritually worthwhile, or rather inexplicable and tedious?

5. Do you read from the Bible at home with any regularity? How do you choose which passages to read? Who or what encouraged you in this practice? In what ways do you find this practice helpful? Do you take breaks?

6. Do you read the lectionary selections at home before worship? When did you begin this practice? Is it always helpful? Sometimes? (Never?)

7. Have some fun designing an awful lectionary.

1 ■ The Design of the Lectionary

> Now on that same day two of them were going to a village
> called Emmaus. . . . Then beginning with Moses and all the
> prophets, he interpreted to them the things about himself
> in all the scriptures.
>
> Luke 24:13, 27

How the Lectionary Reads the Bible

The Revised Common Lectionary is a three-year cycle of biblical
readings. Most worldwide users of the Revised Common Lectionary traverse the three years together: through most of 2021, the
year is B; through 2022, the year is C; and in 2023, back to Year
A. The lectionary lasts three years to correspond with the Bible,
in which three New Testament books—Matthew, Mark, and
Luke—narrate details about the life, death, and resurrection of
Jesus Christ. The lectionary takes three years to experience to reflect
the immense length and breadth of the Bible, and to receive the
fullness of the riches of the scriptures.

The Bible is comprised of about seventy individual books that
were prepared by many authors and editors and that encompass
a wide range of topics, historical issues, and religious sensibilities.
The passages that are studied or treasured depend on what interests
the readers. When we read the Bible, what are we seeking? How
do we open the scriptures? For example, when encountering

Genesis 1, are we looking for science, poetry, faith, God? If we care mostly about ancient Near East history, or at least the biblical version of it, our study will be different than if we are searching for examples of spiritual growth. We all read the scriptures through our own lenses. The classic term used to describe this purposeful reading is "the lectionary's hermeneutic."

The hermeneutic of the Revised Common Lectionary is Christological. The selections were made to proclaim the life offered to the world in Jesus Christ and to enrich the faith of worshiping Christians. The idea is that were a worshiper to attend only a single worship service, the Revised Common Lectionary readings would provide enough of Jesus Christ that God's love was proclaimed and God's Spirit experienced. Every Sunday is centered in God's gift of salvation through Christ. Each week the lectionary intends to awaken and nurture faith, thus meeting its goal even for the many believers who attend worship only about once a month. Seen this way, the lectionary takes not three years, but a single Christological Sunday.

Given that the hermeneutic of the Revised Common Lectionary is Christological, it is clear that much of the Bible will not be appointed for Sunday reading. Such passages may be illuminating to the theologian, interesting to the historian, or beloved by some readers, but they are not central to the faith. Consider for example Leviticus 11, which details ancient Israelite dietary laws. The apostle Peter's dream in Acts 10 counseled Christians not to consider some foods unclean, and so such food regulations have no place in a Christological lectionary. However, Christians of good will have not always agreed on what scriptural passages should be orally proclaimed and intelligibly received each week by the motley group of the assembled believers.

The Four Gospels on Sunday

The Revised Common Lectionary is a Sunday lectionary, meant for use in communal worship on the first day of the week. (See more about this in chapter 5.) The Revised Common Lectionary also provides a set of readings for the Church's most celebratory feasts, which might not fall on a Sunday. Christmas Eve, Christmas Day, Epiphany, Maundy Thursday, Good Friday, Easter Eve, and Ascension are the primary Christological festivals of the liturgical year, and each has an assigned set of texts. Other Christological days are the Presentation of the Lord, the Annunciation of the Lord, the Visitation of Mary to Elizabeth, Holy Cross, and All Saints. Most of these days celebrate the mystery of Christ by focusing on an event in the life of Jesus.

The primary reading for each lectionary set comes from one of the four Gospels.[3] The tradition among many Christians to stand for the reading of the Gospel supports this principle with ritual action. Although the Gospels tell us about the ministry of Jesus, much of what interests a current biographer appears to have been of no concern to the authors of the Gospels. Rather, the four

---

3. For critical commentary, see Gordon W. Lathrop, *The Four Gospels on Sunday: The New Testament and the Reform of Christian Worship* (Minneapolis: Fortress Press, 2012).

Gospels are records of the faith of four different groups of early believers, and the texts demonstrate how their memories of the life, death, and resurrection of Jesus testified to their belief in him. So it is that some preachers occasionally say, not "Jesus said," but "As Matthew wrote."

The Gospel with the most developed understanding of the meaning of Jesus's life, death, and resurrection for the world is the Gospel according to John. Writing in about the year 100, several generations after the life of Jesus, the author of the fourth Gospel proclaims that Jesus is the Word of God, God's incarnation on earth, the very Son of God. It is in John 18:4–5 that the Roman soldiers, coming to arrest Jesus, fall down before him when he calls out *Ego eimi,* "I am," which is the Greek form of YHWH, the Hebrew name of the Holy One. Since the second century, theologians have likened John to the eagle who flies highest and sees furthest. Many Episcopal churches crafted their reading desk (lectern) in the form of an eagle: just as John preaches the faith of the Church, so an eagle holds the Bible. The Revised Common Lectionary appoints John for various times throughout the liturgical year, but most significantly on Christmas Day, some of the Sundays of Lent, Maundy Thursday, Good Friday, Easter, Ascension, and Pentecost. These selections follow the pattern called *lectio selecta,* passages selected to fit the day's focus.

On Sundays throughout the three years, most selections follow the pattern called *lectio continua,* readings chosen sequentially from what are called the three synoptic (or seen together) Gospels. The synoptic Gospels according to Matthew, Mark, and Luke are in some ways similar to each other, yet are quite different from the text in John.

Year A features the Gospel according to Matthew. Written in about the year 80 CE for Jewish Christians, Matthew likens Jesus to Moses by preaching, "Be perfect, therefore, as your heavenly Father is perfect" (Matt. 5:48). In Matthew, Jesus perfects the Law. Year B attends to the Gospel according to Mark. When this earliest Gospel was written in about 70 CE, believers were expecting an imminent end of world: "Keep awake," says Jesus to the disciples (Mark 13:35). In Mark, the Messiah is hidden in his death and at the empty tomb. Year C features the Gospel according to Luke. Written in about 90 CE for Gentile Christians, the narrative describes Jesus as the healer of all people, a storyteller who announces God's forgiveness: "Be merciful, just as your Father is merciful" (Luke 6:36). In Luke, Jesus is the Savior of the world. The diversity presented by the four Gospels clarifies why the Revised Common Lectionary features all four: we need a year of "Be perfect;" we must be continually prodded to "Keep awake;" we discover our need to "Be merciful;" and in Jesus Christ, we encounter the very being of God.

The First Reading

The sacred books written in Hebrew by Jews were adopted by Christians and honored as also their Word of God. Traditionally this group of books was called the Old Testament, although for various reasons some Christians prefer an alternate designation, such as the Hebrew Bible, the Hebrew Scriptures, or the First Testament. For most Sundays and feasts, the Revised Common Lectionary appoints a reading from these books to complement, to provide background for, or to present a parallel to the Gospel reading. When in the 50s Paul wrote that Christ "died for our sins in accordance with the scriptures, . . . and that he was raised on the third day in accordance with the scriptures" (1 Cor. 15:3–4), he meant the Hebrew Scriptures, as the Christian Scriptures were not written yet. Using a Christological hermeneutic, Christian theologians see a continuity between the Jewish and Christian Scriptures, and in Jesus Christ, God offers one way that divine promises to the ancient Israelites are kept.

Over the centuries two different ways for Christians to value the Old Testament were developed. In the fourth century, the Christians of Alexandria in North Africa stressed the spiritual meaning of the texts and related them to stories about Jesus. Meanwhile, the Christians of Antioch in current Turkey preferred attending to the historical development of the Jewish people as told in the Hebrew Bible. The Revised Common Lectionary honors both methods. During the non-festival half of the year, beginning on the Sunday after Trinity and continuing until the end of the liturgical year, the Revised Common Lectionary provides two different sets of Old Testament readings. Some denominations specify a preferred set, some preachers have strong opinions about which set is better, and some homiletical guides deal with only one of the two sets.[4] It is preferable to follow the logic of one of the two sets, rather than to toggle between them.

In accord with the Alexandrian view, what is called in the Revised Common Lectionary the complementary set always connects the first reading with the Gospel, thus providing weekly continuity between the readings. The complementary set values the Hebrew Scriptures with a specifically Christian hermeneutic, stressing the relationship between God's word to the Jews and God's word incarnate in Christ. According to the Antiochian view, what the Revised Common Lectionary calls the semicontinuous set presents a condensed overview of the Old Testament. The readings in Year A come from the Pentateuch, to correspond with Matthew's interest in Judaism; the readings in Year B come from the monarchical histories, to correspond with Mark's image of Jesus as the anointed one; and the readings in Year C come from the prophets, to correspond with Luke's interest in justice for the poor.

During the six Sundays of Easter each year, the first readings come not from the Old Testament, but from the Acts of the Apostles. Though a reading from the Old Testament sees the triune God active in the world before the incarnation of Jesus Christ, a reading from Acts sees that in the healings, the preaching, and the community of the early disciples, the triune God is continuing

---

4. The volume of *Revised Common Lectionary, Episcopal Edition* (New York: Church Publishing, 2007) prints both sets of Old Testament readings, with the complementary set printed directly before the gospel readings and the semicontinuous set printed as the first of the readings of the day.

the work of Jesus Christ. Some users of the Revised Common Lectionary, however, have developed a list of selections from the Old Testament also for these Sundays of Easter, in which case the reading from Acts supplants what the Revised Common Lectionary suggests as the second reading.[5]

A Response from the Psalms

Next, the Revised Common Lectionary lists a passage from the Psalms, which is not a fourth reading, but rather the assembly's response to the first reading or to the day's focus.[6] This response can be chanted or sung in many ways. By means of the psalm response, the Revised Common Lectionary gives to all worshipers the privilege of speaking the Word of God. Both the complementary and the semicontinuous sets of Old Testament readings have been assigned psalms appropriate to their content.

The Second Reading

The second reading is taken from the writings in the New Testament, most of which are epistles written during the first or early second century either to congregations of Christians located around the Mediterranean Sea or to specific individuals. At festival times,

---

5. See Appendix D, "Alternative Readings for the Easter Season: A Proposal to the CCT (2002)," *The Revised Common Lectionary,* 211–14.

6. See Appendix F, "Principles for Psalm Selection in The Revised Common Lectionary (1992)," *The Revised Common Lectionary*, 217.

the second reading is chosen *lectio selecta* to correspond with the day's focus. On standard Sundays, the second reading is chosen more or less by *lectio continua.* Some of these texts were penned several decades before the writing of the Gospels and exemplify the Christian principle that the Word of God, spoken in ancient times, is applicable to the lives of believers in the present.

When the second reading is marked by *lectio continua,* the very book from which the readings are taken was chosen with attention to the liturgical year. For example, during the weeks of Easter in Year B, the second readings come from 1 Peter, which speaks explicitly about the life of those baptized into Christ. During the Easter season in Year C, the second readings come from the Book of Revelation. True to the Christological intention of the Revised Common Lectionary, the selections from Revelation avoid all its gory details and highlight instead the worship of the redeemed at the end of time as characterizing the praise of all Christians thanks to Easter.

The Annual Structure of All Three Years

The Revised Common Lectionary continues Christian tradition by granting highest significance to the annual feasts of Christmas and its attendant Sundays (more on this in chapter 4) and to Easter and its accompanying days (more on this in chapter 5). In the Revised Common Lectionary, the Sundays between Epiphany, which concludes the Christmas season, and Ash Wednesday, which begins the Easter season, are designated as Sundays after the

Epiphany. The Sundays that follow Pentecost until the close of the liturgical year are designated as Sundays after Pentecost.

Proposals for Replacements

Because some Christians judge that the Revised Common Lectionary does not include selected passages that they deem essential for contemporary faith, several alternative lectionary sets have been proposed. Most well-known are the Seasons of Creation, which in their fullest form, as developed by Christians in Australia, replace the Revised Common Lectionary readings for four weeks of earth-focused readings.[7] Some liturgical planners have retained the Revised Common Lectionary readings but have added to them the ecological interest of the Seasons. Any effort toward such replacements discovers that specific parallels to many contemporary issues cannot be found in the Bible. Thus the Church is thrown back once again to its age-old hermeneutical question: how does the Bible speak to the Church today?

An Example: The Third Sunday After Epiphany, Year C

We can now examine one Sunday's texts, to see the design of the Revised Common Lectionary unfold. Since the lectionary is Christological in intent, we always begin any lectionary study with the Gospel.

Every third year in late January the lectionary arrives at Luke 4:14–21. Narrating the formal beginning of Jesus's ministry, Luke

---

7. For Season of Creation, see www.seasonofcreation.com.

tells the story of Jesus in the synagogue in Nazareth, when he is called forward to read the chosen passage and preach on it. The biblical passage that Luke cites, Isaiah 61:1–2, describes the Jubilee. The Jubilee year, said to take place every fifty years, is considered by scholars a non-historical ideal that urged social transformation to rectify the lives of the poor. No crops were grown—thus rest for workers—all debts forgiven, all slaves freed, all lands returned to their original owner. As if providing the groundwork for a theme central to Luke's writings, the Isaiah passage proclaims that the Spirit of the Lord has inspired the prophet. When Jesus had completed the reading, he said, "Today this scripture has been fulfilled in your hearing."

In this Gospel reading, Jesus, speaking with the Spirit of God, is claiming to be in himself the time of the Jubilee. In Christ, implies Luke, are all debts forgiven, all slaves freed: Jesus embodies the historic hopes for social transformation and universal justice that were expressed in the Jubilee. For the baptized, the reminder of the Jubilee serves as an invitation to live out this hope for the human community. The application of this ancient oracle to Jesus demonstrates the fundamental belief of Christianity, that the promises recorded in the Hebrew Bible are experienced in Jesus Christ. In the Revised Common Lectionary, this Christian hermeneutic is proclaimed in our hearing. It is as if the Jubilee is now, in our assembly in late January.

Since the Revised Common Lectionary had already assigned that Isaiah passage to a Sunday in Advent in Year B, the Old Testament reading to complement Luke 4 is Nehemiah 8:1–3, 5–6,

8–10. The book of Nehemiah narrates some events that took place when the Israelites returned to Jerusalem after their exile in Babylon. The city walls have been rebuilt and became a symbol of Jewish reestablishment of the covenant with God in the Promised Land. In this passage from Nehemiah, all the people—both men and women are mentioned—have gathered to hear the priest Ezra read from the scroll of the word, and they listen devoutly to the book of Moses. Hearing the Word of God, the people are invited to celebrate with joy a shared meal and to provide food for the poor. By appointing this passage to complement Luke 4, the Revised Common Lectionary shows the continuity of Jesus's preaching with the Jewish tradition of reading their scriptures in assembly, and the picture of all the people gathered to hear the word and share a meal can be seen as the Christian assembly listening to the biblical readings and holding Eucharist together.

The psalm is 19, in which verses 1–6 praise the sun of God's creation and verses 7–14 praise the Torah, the poet implying that the sun for the believers is the Word of God, giving light to all creation. You will recognize Psalm 19:10: this word is "more to be desired are they than gold, even much fine gold; sweeter also than honey, and drippings of the honeycomb." We might imagine that the returning Israelites had honey with their bread at their celebrative communal meal.

The second readings during these weeks come from 1 Corinthians, written by Paul in the mid-50s. The passage on this Sunday from chapter 12 is the well-known description of the baptized community as the body of Christ, in which each member plays an essential part in the unity of faith. For Paul, the risen body of Christ is present in the body of the Church, which assembles to read the scripture, baptize, and commune. We are accustomed to this depiction of the Church as the one body of Christ. However, newly presented here by Paul, this imagery would have been heard as profoundly countercultural in a world that separated Jew from Greek, slave from free. The readings imply that we know ourselves to be the body of Christ most clearly when we are gathered for word and sacrament.

The lectionary set for the third Sunday after Epiphany is a stunning example of how three readings interweave to proclaim Christ to the body of Christ gathered for worship on Sunday. In our baptism, also we have been given the Spirit of God. We acclaim Jesus as the Jubilee; we join with ancient Israelites to listen to the word, to celebrate at a shared meal, to provide for those who have no food, and to strive for social justice; we sing of the word as the sun of our world, as much fine gold; and we recognize ourselves to be essential members of the body of the risen Christ. The readings have traversed from ancient awe of the cosmos, to a Jerusalem festival day, to a Sabbath in Nazareth, to our very Sunday gathering. In the gesture of the passing of the peace, believers honor the body of one another, for we are one body in Christ. To this complexity of religious meanings, we join with our Jewish forbears to call out our Amen, and in our time, as those who acclaim Christ as the Jubilee, we turn to the care for all who are needy.

All this, on one Sunday in January. Now, we add appropriate assembly song, an inspiring sermon, substantial intercessions for the needy, a collection for the poor, a shared meal of the Spirit, some carefully chosen art and music, and you have the Revised Common Lectionary on Sunday.

Questions for Reflection and Discussion

1. In the children's picture book, *Noah's Ark,* by Peter Spier, several illustrations depict all the animals that were left outside the ark as the water rises up their legs. Compare this picture with the hermeneutic of the proclamation of the flood story (Genesis 7:1–5, 11–18, 8:6–18, 9:8–13) as appointed in the Revised Common Lectionary for the Easter Vigil.

2. In one sitting, read through the Gospel according to John, to see why the Revised Common Lectionary treats it differently from the synoptic Gospels. What is unique to the fourth Gospel? What strikes you as odd?

3. Which is your favorite Gospel? Why?

4. Can you think of an example of when the Christian interpretation of the Hebrew Bible is in danger of being anti-Semitic? What here is at fault?

5. Can Christians continue to refer to use the term "the Old Testament"? Are other designations better? For what reasons?

6. How can study of the lectionary readings be encouraged among your people?

7. Choose a set of Sunday readings at random, and examine how its lectionary selections work together to proclaim Christ. (Did you choose a set that is upcoming on the calendar?)

2 ▪ The Lectionary Is Ecumenical

> The four living creatures and the twenty-four elders fell
> before the Lamb, . . . They sing a new song: " . . . by your
> blood you ransomed for God saints from every tribe and
> language and people and nation; you have made them to
> be a kingdom and priests serving our God. . . . "
>
> Revelation 5:8–10

Lectionaries Before the Ecumenical Movement

We will now discuss how and why our lectionary is ecumenical
by recalling the lectionary situation around the globe in 1950.

Eastern Orthodox churches, as is their tendency, prize what is
seen as most ancient, and so the one-year lectionary that is mandated for their use derives from their earliest practice. Not in 1950
nor in the present is there any apparent discussion about updating
or replacing it.

The worldwide Roman Catholic Church mandated the use of
a one-year lectionary that had developed over the centuries in the
West.[8] For all Sundays and the many feast days, two scriptural
readings were designated, one from the apostolic writings and one

---

8. See Martin Connell, "The One-Year Cycle of Readings before
Vatican II," *Guide to the Revised Lectionary* (Chicago: Liturgy
Training Publications, 1998), 14–16.

from the four Gospels. The psalm was represented by several verses, perhaps chanted by a cantor as an introduction to the liturgy.

Most Anglicans and Lutherans employed a one-year two-reading lectionary, including the several-verse introit, which was similar to the Roman Catholic lectionary.[9] Each church had amended the lectionary to suit its denominational preferences. In some jurisdictions, the use of this denominational lectionary was required.

A primary concern of the churches of the Reformation was to encourage fuller knowledge of the Bible. One prominent Swiss reformer urged that the entire Bible, chapter by chapter, be proclaimed at public worship. Not surprisingly, this ideal quickly devolved into a pattern seen in most Protestant churches in 1950: the text for the sermon was freely chosen by the preacher. Many preachers chose to offer preaching series on topics of interest.

It was common that evangelical churches prized lengthy sermons that were based on short passages chosen from scripture by the preacher. In some churches, worshipers followed along with the biblical passage in Bibles that they had brought from home, transferring the model of Bible study classes into their Sunday worship.

Thus in 1950 there was no coordination among the church bodies as to what were the readings for public worship.

---

9. For a summary of the history of the Anglican lectionary, see Marion J. Hatchett, *Commentary on the American Prayer Book* (Minneapolis: Winston Press, 1980), 324–26.

Denominational publishing houses attended only to their own constituency. Yet some interdenominational conversation was beginning. When the restoration of the Triduum of Maundy Thursday, Good Friday, and the Easter Vigil began, liturgical scholars of several denominations met together in their libraries and at conferences, discussing which were the best biblical choices for these liturgies in the present time. Furthermore, while in many places in the world one single denomination was legally mandated, the free exercise of religion in the United States meant that many American Christians became aware of other traditions than their own and grew less hostile than in the past to the practices of other church bodies.

The Effect of the Ecumenical Movement

During the nineteenth century, considerable conversation arose among the churches especially concerning mission fields. Competing Christian groups were confusing to the newly evangelized, and many doctrinal and ecclesiastical differences that had arisen in Europe had little or no pertinence for believers in other parts of the world. These considerations were central in leading to the 1910 World Mission Conference, which is usually cited as the start of the modern ecumenical movement. The word "ecumenical" derives from the Greek word *oikumene*, which means the whole inhabited world, and some Christians were convinced that Christ's call to the whole inhabited world was in some ways being hampered by denominational specificity. Christ's prayer "that they may all be one" (John 17:21) was a rallying call for cooperative, as opposed to competitive, Christian mission. The formation of the World Council of Churches in 1948 enabled some 350 member churches to converse with one another about common concerns and shared resources.

Historic denominationalism was being questioned and not only in mission fields. In the United States, some immigrant churches were losing the distinctive intensity of their origins, since the tradition in which they had once stood in opposition to no longer wielded any local authority. In some predominantly Christian countries, the increasing presence of other world religions challenged church leaders to find ways to witness to their own neighbors. The worldwide phenomenon of Pentecostalism arose outside of existing church structures. Church mergers prized commonality in the faith over historical backgrounds. Increasingly at many seminaries, students studied the scriptures and church history with textbooks written by scholars outside their own denomination. The practice of intermarriage, especially in North America, meant that Christians did not imprison, or indeed execute, persons of other denominations: they married them, and at least in some homes Christians attempted an interchurch household. By the 1970s, many Christian leaders were asking to what degree their historic distinctiveness remained valuable, versus to what extent they ought to welcome a far more ecumenical future. From bishops to married couples the question was: what do we lose, what do we gain, by an interchurch openness?

The Roman Catholic Lectionary for Mass, 1969

From 1962 to 1965, the bishops of the Roman Catholic Church met for the Second Vatican Council. Many substantial reforms and changes in church life were implemented. A decision with monumental effect was the resolution to authorize an entirely new lectionary.[10] According to the much-cited text, the goal was that "the riches of the Bible are to be opened up more lavishly, so that richer fare may be provided for the faithful at the table of God's Word."[11] Since for several centuries the Western Church had imagined that Roman Catholics, in honoring the apostle Peter, focused their attention on ecclesiastical and sacramental matters, while Protestants, in honoring Paul, dedicated their energies on biblical proclamation, it was something of a surprise for the world Church to witness the comprehensive attention that Vatican II gave to scripture. Just as had Anglicans and Protestants, the members of the Roman Catholic design committee benefited from the wealth of ecumenical biblical studies written during prior decades, and to an impressive degree, the committee applied this recent scholarship to their own internal process of reform.

This newly invented Roman lectionary, first promulgated for use in 1969, was a three-year discipline with three readings and a psalm response for each Sunday and for many other feasts. The

---

10. For details of this history, see Normand Bonneau, *The Sunday Lectionary: Ritual Word, Paschal Shape* (Collegeville, MN: The Liturgical Press, 1998), 63–77.
11. *Constitution on the Sacred Liturgy* II, 51.

lectionary as currently mandated for use has seen several small revisions, and some jurisdictions of the Roman Catholic Church have introduced minor regional variations.[12] Several characteristics of the Roman lectionary exemplify that church's preferred spirituality. For example, considerable attention was given to Marian festivals that enhance the Sunday system. The lectionary readings are relatively short, intending to enrich the faith of the communicants, rather than to educate them about the content of all the scriptures. Roman Catholic educators speak of the homily as opening up the scriptures that they may reveal Christ to the baptized. Thus the intention of the Old Testament selections always in some way leads worshipers toward the gospel reading, rather than instructing them in the whole of the Hebrew Bible.

Most important for its design, the Roman Catholic lectionary is a Sunday eucharistic system, designed to uphold the expectation that the faithful participate in the Eucharist every Sunday, as well as on other feasts and days of obligation. The sections of the Bible that are most valued are those that support the eucharistic piety of the baptized. The liturgical calendar itself indicates this reverence for Eucharist. For example, the Sunday after Trinity Sunday is titled the Solemnity of the Most Holy Body and Blood of Christ, still popularly called by its Latin title, Corpus Christi.

---

12. See National Conference of Catholic Bishops, "Differences between the 1992 Canada and 1998 USA Editions of the Sunday Lectionary," *Lectionary for Mass*, Study Edition, volume I (Collegeville, MN: The Liturgical Press, 1998), 1273–83.

An example of the Roman Catholic devotion to the Eucharist is a unit in the summertime of Year B. Since the Gospel according to Mark is the shortest of the synoptics, Year B has space to dedicate five Sundays to the proclamation of John 6. On what Roman Catholics call the seventeenth through twenty-first Sundays in ordinary time, the lengthy Johannine discourse on the bread of life is divided up into five sections. The first set in this unit includes two narratives, Jesus feeding the five thousand with five barley loaves and two fish and Elisha feeding a hundred people with twenty barley loaves. Thus the lectionary honors God's feeding of the people throughout time, recognized homiletically in God's serving up this Sunday's Eucharist. The psalm response includes the well-known prayer "The eyes of all look hopefully to you," and the second reading from Ephesians calls the baptized into "one body and one Spirit."

The focus on Christ as the bread of life continues. On the eighteenth Sunday in ordinary time, where the Gospel refers to Moses and the manna and calls Jesus the true bread from heaven, the Old Testament selection narrates God's sending the manna to the Israelites, and the psalm response calls God's raining down of the manna "heavenly food." On the nineteenth Sunday, Jesus calls himself the bread of life, which all believers are to eat. The complementary first reading tells of Elijah, awakened by an angel and fed food and water, and thus strengthened to walk to Mount Sinai, here called Mount Horeb, to receive the word of the Lord.

Still, the Roman lectionary is not done with John 6. On the following Sunday, Jesus speaks the odd words about eating the flesh of the Son of Man, and to complement this passage, the Old Testament praises Wisdom, inviting us all to come "eat of my food, and drink of the wine I have mixed!" On the final Sunday of this unit, the last verses of John 6 quote the apostle Peter as affirming Christ, who feeds the people with "the words of eternal life," and in complement, the Old Testament quotes Joshua, whose name is the Hebrew version of the Greek name Jesus, calling the Israelites to choose to serve the Lord.

That five consecutive weeks are dedicated to the proclamation of John 6 is not surprising for Roman Catholics. In this and in many other decisions they are enriched at "the table of God's Word."

The Common Lectionary, 1983

Episcopalians and many North American Protestants, including some Presbyterians, Lutherans, Methodists, Disciples of Christ, and members of the United Church of Christ, joined in the praise of the Roman lectionary, and over the 1970s several denominations amended it for their own use, retaining more or fewer of the Roman preferences. By 1978, an interchurch collaboration called the Consultation on Common Texts was formed, for example, to propose a single contemporary English translation of the Lord's Prayer that all churches could agree on. The Consultation took on the project of proposing from among all the denominational versions a single three-year lectionary that would appeal to Anglicans and at least some Protestant churches. Among other advantages, an ecumenical lectionary would be appreciated by publishing houses, which could stop juggling slightly different lectionary systems in their exegetical and homiletical resources.

The Common Lectionary appeared in 1983.[13] The idea was to retain as much as possible of the Roman lectionary, while making alterations in as few places as was deemed necessary for Anglican and Protestant use. Thus nearly all the Roman Gospel readings were retained, while the second readings were lengthened, adding considerably to the writings of especially Paul. Many of the Roman Catholic feasts and solemnities were omitted. Because most Protestants did not include the books of the Apocrypha in their Bibles, the Common Lectionary provided options for the Roman's apocryphal readings.

The most significant alteration concerned the Old Testament selections. Agreeing to retain Old Testament readings that coordinated with the Gospel reading for the festival seasons of the year, for the remainder of the three years the Common Lectionary presented as the first readings a semicontinuous reading of the Hebrew Bible. The hope was that such exposure to the Old Testament would instruct the faithful in a sense of the whole Bible. The result was that for half the year, the Common Lectionary listed three readings that had no relationship to each other, since the selections from the Old Testament, the apostolic writings, and

---

13. *Common Lectionary: The Lectionary Proposed by the Consultation on Common Texts* (New York: Church Hymnal Corporation, n.d.). Appendix A in *The Revised Common Lectionary*, 163–83, includes the original "Introduction to Common Lectionary (1983)."

the Gospels were each semicontinuous. In Protestant practice, it was often the case that only one of the three readings would be proclaimed at worship, and it might not be the Gospel. Thus the lack of coordination among the readings was not seen as a serious pastoral issue.

Understandably, in the years after the publication of the Common Lectionary, many people voiced their responses to it. Feminist worshipers urged that a revision include more biblical references to women. Many Episcopalians and Lutherans indicated that for hermeneutical reasons, they would not adopt a lectionary in which the first reading had no relationship to the Gospel. Episcopalians, who were canonically required to proclaim all three readings, judged that three unconnected biblical passages would be problematic. Thus the Consultation on Common Texts went back to work.

The Revised Common Lectionary, 1992

In the Revised Common Lectionary we encounter a strikingly ecumenical package.[14] In many ways the Revised Common Lectionary closely resembles its Roman parent. Its Christological hermeneutic is retained. Nearly all the Roman choices for Gospel texts are retained. All the five Sundays of John 6 continue in place, proclaiming Christ as the Bread of Life. There is always the choice for the Old Testament reading to complement the Gospel.

---

14. See Appendix G, "The Reims Statement: Praying with One Voice," *The Revised Common Lectionary*, 219–21.

In other ways the Revised Common Lectionary honored Protestant preferences. In chapter 6 of this study, we will look at the readings added in the Revised Common Lectionary that attend to women. The Revised Common Lectionary retained the practice of longer readings, in the hope that the faithful would read more from the Bible. For examples, the Gospel for Proper 7 in Year A has been lengthened to include the troubling passage (Matt. 10:34–39) in which family members are alienated from each other. The seventh Sunday after Epiphany in Year A includes a fuller listing of the commandments than does the Roman selection. On Proper 12 in Year A, the Roman reading is verses 28–30, but the Revised Common Lectionary reading is the considerably longer passage of verses 26–39. Most significant, given that for half of the year two different sets of Old Testament readings are provided, one complementary and one semicontinuous, each church could choose its preference in this contested matter.

One ecumenical change has been to replace the term "lesson" with "reading." But unfortunately, the churches have not achieved ecumenical consensus in all matters of nomenclature. Denominations use their own titles and numbering systems to designate the same readings. Thus people using exegetical, homiletical, and liturgical resources from several denominations can go out of their minds finding what they are seeking.

An Ecumenical Lectionary for Anglicans

"We believe in one holy catholic and apostolic Church," affirms the Nicene Creed. We pray "for your holy Catholic Church, that we all may be one," that "all who confess your Name may be united in your truth." Many Christians with a passion for the unity of the Church have judged the Revised Common Lectionary to be the most significant ecumenical achievement of the twentieth century.

By listening to biblical scholars and liturgical leaders, and in its early years joined by Roman Catholics who were hopeful that finally all the Western churches could agree on one lectionary, the Consultation on Common Texts produced a compromise document that could serve a wide variety of Christian worship patterns. Indeed, the Revised Common Lectionary has led to some new ecumenical ventures. In some places, clergy groups meet regularly for shared conversation about the texts, thus cultivating deeper ecumenical connections. Denominational publishing houses present their characteristic lectionary interpretations to other church bodies. Far from each preacher personally choosing the sermon text, now Christians of many denominations hear many of the same biblical passages. We can imagine the conversation in some small Protestant church somewhere in the southern hemisphere, thinking about the immense task of revising its lectionary and coming to decide, "That'll be scads of work: let's just adopt the Revised Common Lectionary."[15]

---

15. For a relatively accurate list of the churches worldwide that have adopted or recommended the Revised Common Lectionary, see www.commontexts.org.

The Anglican Communion has always honored the principle of the Via Media, the middle way, holding in polite tension the opposite tendencies expressed by Anglo-Catholics and Episcopal evangelicals. Thus Anglicans might think of themselves as essentially ecumenical, as standing between the Roman Catholic Church and Protestant churches. Thus for Episcopalians, the Revised Common Lectionary can be seen as ideal, honoring both its Roman Catholic parent and its Protestant siblings.[16] Since 2018 not only the Episcopal Church, but also the Church of England has welcomed the Revised Common Lectionary into its practice. There is a much-cited old Christian saying that "how we worship is how we believe." And so we gladly worship in ways as ecumenically as we can, so that we might in our practice be more of the one Church of Jesus Christ around the world. At least in its proclamation of the scriptures, "saints from every tribe and language and people and nation" can unite in the worship of our one God.

Questions for Reflection and Discussion

1. List specific reasons why an ecumenical lectionary is a good idea. List several reasons why it might be problematic. Do you care that the lectionary is ecumenical?

---

16. See Task Force on Liturgical and Prayer Book Revision of the Episcopal Church, "Principles to Guide the Development of Liturgical Texts," October 2019.

2. What are activities in which your parish is involved that are ecumenical in nature? Is it important to the participants that these activities are ecumenical?

3. Did you ever experience ecumenical collaboration as embarrassing? If so, describe what happened.

4. Though based on the worldwide Roman Catholic lectionary, the Revised Common Lectionary is largely a product of first-world northern-hemisphere churches that are accustomed to receiving mandates or direction within their denomination. Such a practice is not the case for all Christians around the globe. Can promotion of the Revised Common Lectionary be accused of being an exercise of white imperialism? If so, what is to be done about that?

5. Is there a danger that too much ecumenical spirit will smother the uniqueness of the Anglican Communion?

3 ■ The Lectionary Is Metaphorical

> Jesus said, "I have said these things to you in figures of speech. . . ."
>
> John 16:25

About Religious Speech

Many of the world's religions agree that things divine are beyond human speech and past human comprehension. For as St. Augustine famously said, "If you understand what you are saying, you aren't talking about God."[17] Even as we speak our worship, we reach beyond words, with bodily gestures, postures, music, art, adornments, vesture, glossolalia, all of which uphold our words with non-words. So although revered Christian theologians composed worthy creeds and crafted doctrinal descriptions, baptized believers were praising God with figures of speech that are outside academic essays about faith.

The Johannine evangelist especially delighted in figures of speech. To call Christ the Word of God is to employ a metaphor. A metaphor is creative. It sheds light, and so we see a new thing. Metaphors transfer a superimposed meaning from one mind to

---

17. Augustine, "Sermons on New Testament Lessons," *A Select Library of the Nicene and Post-Nicene Fathers*, ed. Philip Schaff (New York: Charles Scribner's Son, 1903), VI:263.

another and from the past into the future. To chant that the law of God is better than much fine gold is to rely on metaphor in trying to speak of God. Recall the story in which Moses asks to see God's glory (Exod. 33:18–23). God reminds Moses that no human can see God and live. But God says to Moses, who is standing in the cleft of a rock, "You shall see my back." God's backside? What is this? Well, it's a metaphor. The sacred text speaks as if God has a back that humans can see, as if glimpsing God's backside is all of divine glory that we can handle. We use words that are not, and so we can see what is.

On Proper 12 Year A, metaphor pervades an ostensibly simple parable that equates "the kingdom of heaven" to the yeast that a woman uses in preparing three bushels of flour (Matt. 13:33). Among first-century religious Jews, thus the original hearers of the Gospel according to Matthew, it was common for women to be viewed as, by nature, unclean. As well, the presence of yeast would render unfit for religious use any holy unleavened bread. Three measures of flour, which would equal perhaps as many as 144 cups in our measurement, would yield not, as might be depicted in clip art, three small loaves, but bread for a hundred people, and the amount of flour recalls the story of Sarah preparing bread for the three heavenly visitors (Gen. 18:6).

In this parable that is one verse in length, we are given layers of meaning. "Kingdom" is a biblical metaphor for the realm and might of God; "heaven" is a Hebrew circumlocution that refers to God without saying "God." We will indeed need to read this sentence slowly, since it even begins with metaphors. To the surprise, perhaps shock, of its original hearers, an unclean woman enters the sentence, with unclean yeast, to bake dozens of loaves of regular bread. The Greek, rendered usually as "mixed in with," is literally "hid in." The hearers, who were expecting a description of the majestic power of God, are given instead the unseen yeast in the hands of a woman. What might be first heard as a charming reminder of our grandmother in the kitchen challenges our preconceptions about God, as the words kingdom, heaven, yeast, woman, three measures, and hid all jolt us with another layer of meaning.

The Bible is filled with countless such metaphors. That the author of Acts three times refers to Jesus as having been hanged on a tree (Acts 5:30, 10:39, 13:29) is metaphoric. Roman executions used not a tree, but a pole permanently erected in the ground onto which a cross piece was affixed. The word "tree" recalls the law in Deuteronomy 21:22 describing an ancient practice of execution on a genuine tree, as well as metaphorically seeing this execution pole as generating life for the world. St. Augustine said about his reading of the Bible: "This is what met me: a text lowly to the beginner but, on further reading, of mountainous difficulty and enveloped in mysteries."[18]

The Many Readings for Christmas

The earliest Christian writings by Paul and Mark say nothing of Jesus's birth. By the time of the writing of Matthew and Luke,

---

18. Augustine, *Confessions*, III v. 9, trans. Henry Chadwick (Oxford, UK: Oxford University Press, 1991), 40.

metaphors had entered the Christian imagination, and we encounter these at Christmas. The lectionary set titled Christmas I, usually appointed for Christmas Eve and thus most popularly known, includes Luke's beloved narrative in chapter 2. Acclaiming Jesus as the son of God, Luke states that Jesus was a descendent of King David—oddly, as if through Joseph—since in the cultures of the ancient Near East, the monarch was viewed as a son of the deity. To get Joseph and Mary, residents of Nazareth, to Bethlehem, the city of David, the narrative engages the work of the Roman emperor, who by ordering a societal census unwittingly brought about Jesus's birth in the city of David. That Luke pictures Mary as pregnant and delivering her child is a second characteristic of Luke's writings, which include considerable attention to women. The birth narrative continues with the Lucan concern for the poor, as the angelic announcement comes to shepherds, who were lower class and ritually unclean workers, thus symbolic of the poor to whom the Savior comes.

The Lucan account calls Jesus Savior, Messiah, and Lord and is supported by the first reading from Isaiah 9. Its oracle anticipates the coming of one who is to be named Wonderful Counselor, Mighty God, Everlasting Father, and Prince of Peace. For Christians, these honorifics suggest the mystery of the one mighty triune God, Father, Prince, and Counselor. A part of this oracle that may be disturbing to contemporary hearers is that the joy at this birth is likened to the joy of warriors dividing plunder after a military victory—and this to honor the Prince of Peace! In the communal response to this reading, Psalm 96 praises our God as Creator, king, and judge. We call our song "a new song," for Jesus is born. The second reading on Christmas I is a passage from Titus, a late first-century epistle addressed to residents of Crete. Perhaps the letter singled out Crete because of its bad reputation—see Titus 1:12—but during worship, the letter addresses us, calling us, even during this celebrative time of excess, to "lives that are self-controlled, upright, and godly."

The lectionary set titled Christmas III, usually assigned to Christmas Day, is wholly different. The primary reading is the prologue of the Gospel according to John, a poetic praise of Christ as the Word of God, the light of the cosmos, by whom the worlds were created, and who continues to give life to the world. By beginning this Gospel with the phrase "In the beginning," the fourth evangelist connects the arrival of Jesus with the creation of the world in Genesis. This cosmic light can render us all to become children of God.

The first reading on Christmas III complements John 1 by announcing that "your God reigns." On Christmas Day God's "holy arm" brings joy to all the nations: this is God we are praising. In Psalm 98, God's arm has won the victory, and we laud the arrival of the divine judge, who will establish a world of righteousness. The second reading for Christmas Day, a selection from the beginning of the book of Hebrews, calls Christ God's Son, the heir of all things, through whom God created the world and who now reigns with the divine Majesty. Christ is "the exact imprint of God's very being." Thus celebrating Christmas is about seeing God.

On Christmas Eve we heard from Luke the endearing story of Bethlehem, and on Christmas Day, we encountered the splendor of the cosmic Christ from John. But the lectionary is not done with the birth of Jesus. On Epiphany, January 6, the lectionary appoints the birth story from the Gospel according to Matthew. Here, men take center stage: the annunciation has come not to Mary, but to Joseph; King Herod investigates the birth of a rival monarch; and the chief priests and scribes advise the king. Perhaps even all the magi, important religious and cultural figures who honor this birth, were men. Their gifts, which would be extremely odd as literal presents, are religious symbols: gold denoting Jesus as a king; frankincense and myrrh being sweet-smelling resins used in offerings to deities and status burials. In Matthew, the reader encounters Jesus as a king destined for death.

The first reading on this last of three Christmas liturgies is an oracle from Isaiah 60 that praises the glory of God appearing like a light over the earth. It is likely that Matthew borrowed from this Isaiah poem the mention of gold and frankincense, hoping that the Jewish audience would recognize this reference, when "the wealth of the nations" would be offered in praise. Psalm 72 praises this king who will bring justice to the poor and peace of all. The reason that Christian tradition has called the magi kings comes from Psalm 72, which speaks of kings bringing gifts to this newly acclaimed king. The second reading on Epiphany is from Ephesians 3, an apostolic writing that repeatedly cites the power of light over darkness. The selected passage speaks of "the mystery" of God, hidden for ages, but now made known in Jesus Christ. So once again the lectionary leads the Church through cosmic imagery into divine mysteries.

In summary, Christmas requires our attention to three different metaphoric scenes: to speak of Jesus coming to a world filled with poverty, see Luke; to encounter Christ as the light of the cosmos, see John; to place Jesus Christ in the world of powerful authorities, see Matthew. In the Revised Common Lectionary, Christmas is like a three-act play, with the Savior featured differently in each.

The Many Readings for Holy Week and Easter

One problem with popular movies that depict the gory details of some version of Jesus's passion and death is that the audience is led to assume that the film is based on simple facts. But since the scriptures do *not* narrate one simple story, neither does the Revised Common Lectionary. Worshipers are offered glimpses of the mystery, told with figures of speech. The Revised Common Lectionary supports the move in the twentieth century to revive the liturgies of the Triduum, and these liturgies of Maundy Thursday, Good Friday, and the Vigil of Easter rely on metaphor to tell the meaning of Christ's passion, death, and resurrection.

On Maundy Thursday, the Triduum expands on the term "the body of Christ" several ways. The second reading cites Paul's description of Jesus's last meal before his death—"This is my body." But the gospel reading from John 13 features another vision of "the body of Christ." On Maundy Thursday, Jesus's body is there as he washes his disciples' feet, as are the bodies of all the disciples. The first reading from Exodus 12 sets up a parallel between the

Passover meal of the Israelites and the Eucharist celebrated by the Church. Thus the body of the lamb, the body of Christ shared, the body of Christ kneeling before the disciples, the body of Christ now seen in one another's feet: the metaphor keeps turning, showing yet another side of the mystery.

The Triduum continues on Good Friday. Through the centuries, many Christians have kept Good Friday as a day of deepest mourning, and in some places the worship services and attendant rituals have striven for verisimilitude in describing the sufferings of Jesus. However, not the Revised Common Lectionary, in which the synoptic accounts of Jesus's passion and death that deal more graphically with Jesus's sufferings are appointed for the previous Sunday. By proclaiming on Good Friday the triumphant account of Jesus's passion and death from the Gospel according to John, the Revised Common Lectionary relies once again on metaphor. In John, when being asserted, Jesus calls out, "I AM." In John, Jesus is not mute, but debates truth with Pilate. In John, Jesus attends to his mother and beloved disciple from the cross. There are no references to Jesus's bodily misery; rather, he drinks the wine, his legs are not broken. His burial in a garden is yet another metaphor. Corpses were not buried in gardens in the Roman Empire. The fourth evangelist is offering a figure of speech: Jesus's death brings forth life. That Jesus is buried with a hundred pounds of spices signifies that Jesus is king.

For the first reading on Good Friday, the selection from Isaiah 52–53 likens Jesus to a young plant, a man despised, a lamb readying for slaughter, a silent ewe, a sin offering. Take your pick—there are lots of metaphors. In Psalm 22, the suffering one is surrounded by packs of dogs and is laid in the dust of death. Yet at the end, all who are dead will bow down before this one: there we are, kneeling down with the arresting police. In the second reading from Hebrews, two opposite images are presented. Christ is both the lamb whose blood will save, and he is the great priest who performed the sacrifice. No single metaphor can say it all; each metaphor is opened up by its opposite.

Then comes the third part of the Triduum, first Eucharist of Easter, the Vigil, held sometime on Saturday night. What is the resurrection of Jesus Christ like? It is like the creation of the world (Genesis 1); rescue from the flood (Genesis 7–9); Isaac's escape from sacrifice (Genesis 22); the Israelites' freedom from slavery in Egypt (Exodus 14, 15); a free feast on the mountaintop (Isaiah 55); wisdom, a divine female, inviting us to faith (Baruch or Proverbs); clean water and a new spirit (Ezekiel 36); the dry bones restored to life (Ezekiel 37); return to our homeland (Zephaniah 3); and baptism (Romans 6). The hope is that all these metaphors can help us believe.[19]

With a biblical diversity that we have come to expect of the Revised Common Lectionary, the Vigil of Easter and the festival

---

19. *Evangelical Lutheran Worship* and the Presbyterian *Book of Common Worship* add to this list several readings that were important images of the Resurrection in the early Church: Jonah's three days in the fish, the three children in the furnace, and the valley of the dry bones.

service on Easter Day present two different biblical narratives of the Resurrection. Depending on the year, the synoptic account from Matthew, Mark, or Luke is proclaimed at one of the services, and each year John 20 is proclaimed at the other service.[20] The four Gospel accounts involve different characters and varied time-lines, for these are not eyewitness newspaper reports. Rather, in New Testament fashion, they are proclamations of the faith of the Church, and we join with Mary Magdalene as she calls out, "I have seen the Lord."

The Many Readings for Pentecost

For the third of the central festivals of the liturgical year, the Revised Common Lectionary once again provides texts marked by metaphor. For the Day of Pentecost in Year A, the gospel reading is from John 20. Though it is still the day of Christ's resurrection, Jesus appears to his disciples, extends to them divine peace, and breathes the Holy Spirit onto them. The evangelist is here repeating the imagery from Genesis 2, in which God breathes life into the newly formed creature of dust. An option for the Gospel reading is a short passage from John 7, in which the Spirit is likened

---

20. The Revised Common Lectionary and the Episcopal practice appoint the synoptic account of the Resurrection at the Vigil and the Johannine account on Easter Day. However, in *Evangelical Lutheran Worship* (2006) p. 31, and in the Presbyterian *Book of Common Worship* (2018) p. 298, the gospel readings are reversed, so that John is proclaimed throughout the entire Triduum and the synoptic accounts, matching Passion Sunday, on Easter Day.

to rivers of living water, thus celebrating the Christian focus on baptism.

To complement the Gospel reading, the lectionary presents several options from which to choose. One possibility is the well-known narrative from Acts 2. Told quite differently than in John, and marked by Luke's extraordinary narrative skill—we hear about even the charge of drunkenness—the Spirit is blown into a room where the believers are gathered fifty days after the Resurrection. The Jewish Pentecost commemorated God's appearance in fire on the mountaintop of Sinai. Here in Acts, the fire appears on the foreheads of each disciple, denoting God's gift of the divine Spirit to each person and around the whole inhabited world. A second option is the narrative from Numbers 11 in which the spirit that God had given to Moses was dispersed among the seventy elders. The story includes the somewhat comic account of Eldad and Medad, who apparently in an unorthodox manner also received the spirit. We smile as we realize that even back then, believers quarreled over authority in the community. The third option is a passage from 1 Corinthians. Paul describes the ideal Christian community, in which the Spirit, which is granted to all believers through baptism, is given to each individual for unique service to the whole. The psalm response includes the verse in which the Hebrew noun *ruah* is usually in this psalm translated as "spirit." In this biblical passage, the Spirit of God is active first and foremost in the creation of the world.

Thus Pentecost A offers us the breath of the Risen Christ; rivers of water; the fire of Mount Sinai now in the upper room; a mighty wind blowing from God; the seventy elders, Eldad, and Medad each receiving Moses's spirit; the Spirit granted in baptism; and divine life at the world's creation. Pentecost celebrates not only a single historic event, but a rich array of Christian memories and meanings, each vying for our attention as one of the many ways that God's Spirit is given.

And that is only Pentecost in Year A. In Pentecost Year B in the Revised Common Lectionary, the Gospel reading is from John 15 and 16, in which Jesus describes the coming Spirit of truth who will be the divine authority in the community now that Jesus will be absent. That the fourth Gospel calls the Spirit the Greek word *paraklete* is an example of a figure of speech, and translators offer a wide range of terms—counselor, comforter, helper, advocate, friend—to convey the nuances of this odd term. An optional reading is the vision of Ezekiel of the valley of the dry bones, upon which the Spirit comes, so that the bones arise and live. A reading from Romans speaks of the Spirit of God living within the believer and teaching us how to pray. It is as if the Spirit coming in baptism becomes a divine voice speaking within us.

In Pentecost Year C, the Gospel reading is from John 14, an early Christian testimony to the Trinity of the Father, the Son, and the Spirit of truth. This Spirit will lead the faithful into greater works even than Jesus himself performed. Other Year C options include the legend in Genesis 11 of the tower of Babel, chosen to contrast with Luke's narrative in Acts. In Babel, God introduces many languages to complicate cooperative living and bring about social divisions; in Jerusalem after the Resurrection, the many languages serve to speak God's Spirit to the whole world.

This treasury of biblical passages appointed for the Day of Pentecost illustrate the pattern of the Revised Common Lectionary: offer as many as possible of the biblical riches, toward the enrichment of faith. Assume that it will take at least three years to explore all these images. During and outside worship, teach those who are baptized these metaphors, so that hearing Acts 2, they know that the wind is not merely a wind: it is rather the creative power of the Resurrection realized within the community. Each biblical passage sheds some light on the mysteries of the faith. Each relies on a figure of speech that arises from other significant biblical passages. We might think of the Revised Common Lectionary readings, not as episodes in biblical history, but rather as many varied spiritual adventures in the heights and depths of religious revelation.

That the Revised Common Lectionary relies so much on biblical figures of speech may be jarring to those who assume that the church year means solely to narrate the life of Jesus. However, although the Scriptures record surprisingly few hard facts about Jesus, Christians have found throughout both Testaments countless pictures of salvation that fill up the three years of the lectionary. Sunday after Sunday, these metaphors provide titles to praise this Jesus, avenues we walk down together, gems that show attributes of our God. The lectionary is indeed much fine gold.

Questions for Reflection and Discussion

1. Should religion be simple? Why or why not?

2. Which Christmas reading do you prefer, Luke 2 or John 1? Why?

3. Some Christians begin their single Christmas service with Luke 2, and then proceed with the readings for Christmas III, which features John 1. Is this use of two Gospel readings a useful plan?

4. Compare a synoptic account of Jesus's passion and death with that in John's Gospel. Select details of each that you treasure.

5. The passion accounts in Matthew and John include verses that some people find anti-Semitic. What should the lectionary do about this?

6. A haiku is a three-line poem, usually about nature, with five syllables in the first line, seven in the second, and five in the third. Write a haiku about the Easter Vigil.

7. Choose your favorite three biblical passages for Pentecost out of the eleven that are suggested in the Revised Common Lectionary. Why do you like these? What is your single most favorite metaphor for the Holy Spirit?

4 ▪ The Lectionary Is Historic

> . . . because of all that was written in this letter, and of what they had faced in this matter, and of what had happened to them, the Jews established and accepted as a custom for themselves and their descendants and all who joined them, that without fail they would continue to observe these two days every year, as it was written and at the time appointed.
>
> Esther 9:26–27

Historicity in Religions

Religion is sometimes defined as a tradition of communal value. We read in the story of Esther that since religion is a tradition, its past is to be reiterated in the present and the future. In some religious practices, the communal tradition is so essential to the entire enterprise that there is strong resistance to any change whatsoever. It is as if religion is the past restored and celebrated, as if enlightenment and salvation come into the present from that past. Houses of worship may resemble museums where only the past is honored. For some Christians, the historic liturgy, or at least the current sense of what was traditional practice, is the immovable foundation in the structure of faithful worship in the present.

Yet the invention and adoption of first the Roman Catholic lectionary and then the Revised Common Lectionary exemplify the readiness of the Church in the West to alter past practice for the future. Before we address the ways in which the Revised Common Lectionary reflects a contemporary worldview (in the next chapter), it is useful first to consider the ways that the three-year lectionary honors Christian history and, at least to some degree, meets the classic call for religions to maintain traditions of holiness.

The Historic Calendar

Historians tell us that before the time of literacy, humans gave communal order to society by attending to the cosmic movements of the sun, moon, and planets. As people realized that such an order existed, they judged it prudent to mimic this order by means of annual celebrations. In the northern hemisphere, the two primary religious rituals were set at the spring equinox and the winter solstice. We excavate in and around Stonehenge, staggered at the magnitude of the centuries-long dedication to its rites that ordered the earth by honoring the sky. The two preeminent Christian festivals that the Revised Common Lectionary maintains as Easter and Christmas continue the tradition in the northern hemisphere of attending to the spring equinox and the winter solstice.[21]

---

21. Details are provided in Andrew B. McGowan, *Ancient Christian Worship: Early Church Practices in Social, Historical, and Theological Perspective* (Grand Rapids: Baker Academic, 2014), 217–60.

In the ancient Near East, the spring equinox was of immense importance. Barren winter was over, and the time of growing the community's food had come. By equalizing the hours of day and night, the equinox demonstrated harmony in the earth. For the Israelites, the Passover came to be scheduled in relation to the spring equinox and full moon that followed, thus celebrating not only the life of the cosmos and the life of the fields, but also the life of the community. Still today, Jews keep Passover (Pesach in Hebrew) at the first full moon after the spring equinox, thus inviting the religious community to join in the harmony of the cosmos.

Early Christians continued to observe the Jewish Passover, adding the resurrection of Jesus Christ onto its list of celebrations. Yet during the second century theologians disputed: should the annual celebration of the Resurrection follow the usual Christian pattern, that Sunday is the foremost day of religious gatherings? Sunday won: the decision was to keep Easter on the first Sunday after the first full moon after the spring equinox, thus giving an explicitly Christian slant to the historic honoring of the skies. Christians continue to compute the date of Easter in this traditional way, according to which Easter can occur anytime between March 22 and April 25. That the Eastern Church settles on a different date from the Western Church arises because the two traditions use different astronomical calendars for their computations. Given the many biblical uses of "forty days" as a time of preparation, the Revised Common Lectionary maintains the historic practice of setting Ash Wednesday and Lent as the forty days before Easter, and given the Jewish dating of Pentecost as a festival on the fiftieth day after Passover, the Revised Common Lectionary continues to keep Easter as fifty days long.

One way that the Revised Common Lectionary embodies past traditions is by restoring the three-day celebration of the Triduum. By restoring the great Three Days of Maundy Thursday, Good Friday, and the Vigil of Easter, as no longer merely a preference for a few, but rather as the foremost manner for the whole Church to keep Christ's passion, death, and resurrection, the three-year lectionary makes the Church's history a source of contemporary meaning. That the Church of future centuries will resemble the Church of the fourth century more than that of the nineteenth makes the commitment to celebrate the Triduum a fitting Easter solution in our neopagan times. What for centuries was lost has been discovered as still full of life for years to come.

During the Roman Empire, the winter solstice had become the primary annual religious and social festival, a several-day blowout of feasting and partying. That the sun was seen for a minute longer than the day before, thus imagined as the birthday of the sun, became a sign that death was giving way to life. By the third century, some Christians began to introduce some holiness to this raucous festival by dedicating the holiday to a commemoration of the birth of Jesus. Because of the shifting of calendars over the centuries, the social festival, although not the literal winter solstice, has moved to December 25, the Christian Christmas. Perhaps because Christmas was a relatively late addition to the liturgical calendar, perhaps because of the popularity of the pagan celebration, Christians did not move the festival to a nearby Sunday. Although Christmas is now of highest religious and social significance, it is interesting to recall that the strict Puritans of the seventeenth century, in rejecting all churchy inventions, did not keep Christmas in any way, and in the Massachusetts Bay colony, all Christmas celebrations of any kind were against the law.

The Revised Common Lectionary maintains the historic connection between the emergence of light at the north's winter solstice and the celebration of the birth of Jesus. We see this clearly in the lectionary reading for Christmas Day, the poem to Christ as the light in John 1. Following early medieval tradition, the Revised Common Lectionary sets Advent as four weeks preparing for Christmas and Christmas itself as lasting twelve days culminating at Epiphany. If Easter is about cosmic life, Christmas is about divine love, and both retain their historic dating in the novel three-year calendar.

The Revised Common Lectionary is a Sunday lectionary, which serves as an example of theologians looking into past tradition for future worship. By the early second century, Sunday had been chosen as the time of the weekly assembly. Over the centuries, especially where Christianity became the state religion, the linking of communal worship with the day of Christ's resurrection was overlooked. Easter became an annual feast, not the weekly event in the Church's worship life. Some Christians gave Sunday an alternate historicity, by seeing the first day of the week as a transferred Jewish Sabbath. Those who designed the three-year lectionaries restored the ancient Christian practice of keeping Sunday as the worship day because on Sunday Christ rose from the dead. In this way also, the novel lectionary was historic. It is perhaps best if "lectionary Christians," living from Sunday to Sunday, avoided using calendars that construe Monday as the first day of the week.

The Lenten Baptismal Focus

In the early centuries of the Church, Easter was the preferred occasion for all baptisms, and the weeks prior to Easter were dedicated to the preparation of baptismal candidates, called catechumens, for their baptism at the Vigil. However, as baptism became a standard rite given to all citizens as infants, Lent lost its baptismal character, and as monasteries, which did not celebrate baptisms, became models of Christian worship, less attention was granted to the many meanings of baptism. Instead, during medieval times, Lent developed as a time to focus on one's sinfulness, to seek forgiveness, and to enact penance, so that one could participate in the annual communion at Easter. In many places, Lent focused on sin by becoming a six-week meditation on the passion of Christ. However, also in this regard, the twentieth century resembled the fourth century, with fewer infants but more adults being presented for baptism. Thus Lent in the Revised Common Lectionary returned to that earlier understanding of the preparation for Easter: not sinners meditating on Christ's passion, but instead catechumens, along with their Christian companions and baptismal sponsors, readying for baptism and baptismal renewal at Easter.

In all three years, the first Sunday of Lent maintains the historic practice of beginning the forty days with the narrative of the temptation of Jesus. Just as Jesus rejected the devil, so at the beginning of the rite of baptism we renounce the forces of Satan. The baptismal focus of Lent continues most clearly during Year A.

On the second Sunday in Lent in Year A, John 3:1–17 presents the conversation between the seeker Nicodemus and Jesus, which speaks of the Spirit of God granted at baptism, the new birth that comes about, the goal of seeing Christ lifted up on the cross, and the salvation of the world. The gospel on the following Sunday, John 4:5–42, is the surprising conversation between the Samaritan woman at the well and Jesus, which proclaims Jesus as "the spring of water gushing up to eternal life," and points to Jesus as the Messiah. The narrative concludes with many Samaritans, who were outsiders to strict Jewish practice, believing that Jesus is the Savior of the world. The gospel on the next Sunday, John 9:1–41, is the narrative of Jesus healing the man born blind and includes the nearly comic interactions between the various characters in the story: who is this Jesus? Can he forgive sin? It was largely this narrative that led early theologians to call baptism enlightenment, as with the man born blind we too are brought to sight by the water of life. The gospel on the fifth Sunday of Lent, John 11:1–45, is the narrative of Jesus raising Lazarus from the grave. Conversing with Lazarus' sisters Mary and Martha, Jesus proclaims that he himself is the Resurrection and the life. The lengthy narratives in Year A have become beloved for many Christians, who see in these Johannine stories the entire Lenten journey, from seeking Jesus in the night and being reborn, to drinking of Christ as the living water, to having our sight restored, to being called out of our graves into the life of the baptized.

Christian Reliance on the Hebrew Bible

Recently, the early Church's adoption of the Hebrew Bible as the foundation on which to build Christian belief has been challenged. Assisted by discoveries in language, history, and archaeology, some students are urged to set aside their Christian identity when studying the Old Testament and to attend solely to the original meaning of the ancient texts. Some Christians judged the title "Old Testament" as pejorative, as if construing the Hebrew Bible as only a precursor to the Christian Scriptures. The Holocaust had exposed a tradition of anti-Semitic interpretation that led some in the Church to reject Christian gloss or appropriation of the Hebrew Bible. Although for centuries churches did not include a reading from the Old Testament during worship, an elaborate hermeneutical system called typology suggested that God's interactions with Israel served solely to prepare the world for God's incarnation in Jesus Christ, and in recent decades some Christians condemned the entire typological enterprise as essentially anti-Semitic. Some Christians sponsored their own seder meals, hoping in this way to honor Jewish religious tradition, despite other Christians and many Jews viewing this practice as historically naïve and an unauthorized commandeering of other people's religious rituals. Clearly, with such issues widely debated, Christian lectionaries had some decisions to make.

The Revised Common Lectionary's response was to continue but to reform the historic practice of Christian reliance on the Old Testament. The Christian Scriptures assume knowledge of the Hebrew Bible; some scholars have called the New Testament a "gloss" on the Old. Christians need to value the Old to understand the New. Even to call Jesus (which is the same name as Joshua) Lord (an Old Testament circumlocution for "God") and Christ (meaning "the anointed one") requires a borrowing from the Hebrew Scriptures. But reform was also essential. In the Revised Common Lectionary, the prophets' railing against the sins of the Israelites is not intending to condemn contemporary Jews, but rather is set parallel to Christ's call to Christians to obey the Word of God. The careful placement of passages from the Old Testament led not to a devaluing of Jewish tradition, but rather a re-valuing of God's irrevocable covenant with the Jews and a religious bonding between Christians and Jews. Similarities were lauded and differences considered in a spirit of interfaith cooperation.

One positive example of the lectionary use of the Old Testament is seen in the figure of Wisdom. Especially during intertestamental times, a tradition of poetry depicted God's wisdom as a kind of goddess in the sky named Wisdom. With her assistance, God created the earth and rules the people, and from her the faithful learn the righteous life. In this genre of poetry, the righteous life was taught by the good woman, and the foolish life by Lady Folly. There has been considerable discussion among scholars about this Wisdom genre: does it testify to goddess worship surviving in

Jewish orthodoxy, or was it merely a poetic device, intended for adolescent boys' education?

In the Revised Common Lectionary, Wisdom appears at the Easter Vigil, in either Proverbs 8 and 9 or Baruch 3. At the Vigil, all Old Testament readings are figures of speech used to proclaim the Resurrection. Thus at this first Eucharist of Easter, Wisdom is the female depiction of Christ, the living book of the commandments of God, the hostess inviting us to her meal of bread and wine. Wisdom is present again on Trinity Sunday in Year C, when in the passage from Proverbs 8 the wisdom of the triune God has created the world. By offering a metaphor for the second person of the Trinity, Proverbs 8 complements the focus on the third person of the Trinity in John 16:12–5, with its focus on the third person of the Trinity. How the Revised Common Lectionary appoints Wisdom demonstrates its commitment to the best of the Church's historic hermeneutic: to honor the Hebrew Bible by seeing in the Jewish tradition a wider swath of God's people receiving the empowering mercy of the divine.

A further example of how the Revised Common Lectionary deals with the Old Testament are the readings appointed for the fourth Sunday in Lent in Year B. Its appointed gospel reading, John 3:14–21, includes what is perhaps the most cited verse in the New Testament, "God so loved the world." Jesus is described as one who must "be lifted up." But what is this "lifting up"? The Johannine author cites the odd narrative in Numbers 21:4–9 in which the Israelites, stricken with snake bite as punishment from God for complaining about their situation in the wilderness, are told to look upon the image of a bronze serpent on a pole. It seems that a pre-Israelite worship of Asherah, a Canaanite goddess displayed on a pole, had found its way into Jewish memory, and despite our sense that this resembles idolatry, the pagan symbol of holiness serves to heal God's people. The Revised Common Lectionary maintains the historic pattern that Numbers 21 be tied to John 3, the bronze serpent to the crucified Christ, so that worshipers see the two poles on which God offers salvation.

A lectionary set that is somewhat more complicated is the fourth Sunday of Advent in Year A. The gospel reading is Matthew 1:18–15, the annunciation of Jesus's birth to Joseph. In the Matthean text, as proof to Joseph that God intends this pregnancy, the angel cites a passage from Isaiah anticipating the birth of a child named Emmanuel, which means "God is with us." In the original Greek of the book of Matthew, the woman in verse 23 is a virgin. However, in the original Hebrew text of Isaiah, the expectant woman is not described as a virgin. This set of readings typifies the complexity of tying the two Testaments together. As we become aware of the problems of translating Hebrew into Greek into English, we can be grateful for what is a most helpful parallel between Isaiah 7 and Matthew 1: that throughout time, God is with us, and that whether in a societal disaster in the ancient Near East, in Joseph's concern over an unexplained pregnancy, or in any current distress, God is with us.

In the present time, perhaps the most troubling use in Christian lectionaries of the Old Testament are those passages in the passion narratives that many worshipers view as anti-Semitic.

Contemporary biblical scholars have demonstrated that the four Gospels present incomplete and conflicting accounts of Jesus's trials and execution.[22] Yet what worshipers encounter in Matthew 27:25 is "the crowd" accepting for its posterity responsibility for Jesus's death and, most especially, in the New Revised Standard Version (NRSV) of John 18–19, twenty-one times that the Greek noun *Ioudaioi* (literally, "the Judeans") is cited negatively. Many Christians are helped by consulting other translations of John, in which for example "the crowd" or "the temple authorities" render the Greek with a noun more fitting to the narrative context.[23] Awareness of the antagonistic situation between Christians and Jews during the late first century, when the Gospel according to John was written, may help to explain this pattern of speech: for despite the Christian practice of honoring the scriptures as the Word of God, these books were penned by persons at specific times of history, which in some cases differ radically from our own.

In summary we can say that although the Revised Common Lectionary may be seen as a new lectionary, in many essentials it is wholly traditional. The primary festivals of Easter and Christmas come into the twenty-first century from the earliest times, the

---

22. For a comprehensive discussion of the passion narratives, see Raymond E. Brown, SS, *The Death of the Messiah*, vol. 1 and 2 (New York: Doubleday, 1994).

23. For a discussion of the translation issues and an emended Johannine text of the passion narrative, see "Seasonal Rites for the Three Days," *Sundays and Seasons Year A 2020* (Minneapolis: Augsburg Fortress, 2019), 142–5.

Triduum and a baptismal Lent are restored, and the traditional pattern of finding the Christian mystery hidden in the Hebrew Bible is maintained and reformed. Although it is not the intention of the Revised Common Lectionary to teach the Bible, the entire Bible is laid upon the annual calendar, as it has been over the centuries, for Christ to illumine all of our lives, week by week.

Questions for Reflection and Discussion

1. What would be the advantages were the worldwide Church to select a single date for Easter? What are the disadvantages of such a plan?

2. The word "Easter" comes from the name of a pagan goddess of the dawn, "Eoster." Some Christians prefer to refer to the festival as Pascha, thus making the Jewish origins more evident. What is the best way to title our annual celebration of Christ's resurrection?

3. Should churches urge that Christians keep Sunday as Sabbath? How would a Sunday Sabbath function for you?

4. An advertisement in a grocery store seems not to get the point when it states, "It's Lent, eat shrimp." Do you "give up" something for Lent? How else might we keep Lent?

5. Discuss the meaning of the virginal conception of Jesus. Is this an important doctrine for you?

6. Check the tiny marginal notes in the NRSV's New Testament to see the variety of ways that it renders the Greek *adelphoi*, literally "brothers," as contextually appropriate. You will find, for example, all the members of God's family, brothers and sisters, friends,

beloved, believers. When would you judge that a "translation" is actually more like a "paraphrase"?

7. What is something historic in the Church that you wish we could discard? Do your friends and family agree with you about this?

5 ▪ The Lectionary Is Contemporary

> And the one who was seated on the throne said, "See, I am making all things new. . . . "
>
> Revelation 21:5

Newness in Religion

Although, along with other world religions, Christianity has continued to honor the historic, since its inception it has also been open to what is new. The decision for Jews to evangelize Gentiles was a preeminent example of radical change that determined the Church's future, and Galatians and the Acts of the Apostles record interestingly different versions of the first-century debates among Church leaders about whether the community was to develop in surprising, perhaps even upsetting, ways. That Paul wrote to the Church in Corinth correcting their religious meal practice is another illustration that all biblical writings, indeed, sometimes even of different parts of the same book, were written at a certain time toward a specific religious or social purpose. The theological differences between Mark and the later Gospels demonstrate that during successive decades, evangelists felt authorized to speak of Jesus in a way specific to their own time and community. Because society changes, Christians have said that the Word of God must be heard addressing that new situation.

As was the writing of the Bible, so is the reading from the Bible. During worship, reading the Bible is not like reading *Beowulf*. The Jesus-then has to be experienced as the Jesus-now.[24] To see this Christian sense that what is proclaimed weekly from the Bible matters in the present, we can compare which biblical passages have been suggested for the rite of marriage: as the social understanding of the role of spouses changed, so did the readings at weddings. As well, that nineteenth-century Christians in the American north and south disagreed about what to read from the Bible on the issue of slavery ought not to surprise us, since both groups assumed that God was speaking to their own particular situation.

The Revised Common Lectionary continues the classic Christian understanding that through the words of scripture, God is speaking to the present time, and lectionaries are to appoint what appears to be of most significance for believers now. Some decisions are easy to agree upon: none of us includes on Sunday morning the legend in Genesis 6 that describes the race of giants who arose from sexual intercourse between angels and humans. Happily, some contemporary concerns pervade the scriptures: much of the Hebrew Bible speaks of God's intention that communal life be marked by justice for the poor, food for the hungry, and integrity in government, and many of the selections among the lectionary's first readings proclaim this biblical emphasis. In this chapter, we

---

24. John Dominic Crossan, *The Birth of Christianity* (San Francisco: HarperSanFrancico, 1998), 32.

will look at some of the selections made in the Revised Common
Lectionary to affirm God's word addressing the contemporary
world.

For starters, there is the way that recent biblical studies have
influenced the layout of the lectionary. In the second century there
was promulgated the Diatessaron, a harmony of the four Gospels
that eliminated their doublets and contradictions, an effort that
has left its mark on children's Bible study. By the fifth century the
liturgy had replaced use of the Diatessaron with proclamation
from the four separate Gospels, yet with no attempt to distinguish
between them. However, the last two centuries of academic study
of the scriptures has led to great interest in the differences apparent
between books of the Bible, heightening awareness that every book
of the Bible was composed by specific authors in specific times for
specific reasons.

For many Christians, among them the theologians who
designed the three-year lectionaries, these differences illumine,
rather than upset, our reception of the Word. It is best if a lectionary be based upon, rather than dismissive of, scholarly study
of the Bible. Reflecting this contemporary study of the scriptures,
the Revised Common Lectionary features each Gospel in its own
particularity. So, for example, rather than obscure the fact that
the synoptics report that the Last Supper was a Passover meal,
while the Gospel according to John states that the Crucifixion
took place as the Passover lambs were being slaughtered, the
Revised Common Lectionary mines this difference by appointing
the synoptics on Passion Sunday and John on Good Friday, thus

encouraging parish catechesis to explore the meaningful theological differences.

That academic study would enhance rather than detract from believers' reception of the scriptures is evident in the Anglican emphasis on reason as an essential tool for biblical interpretation. Reason helps to guide the Church in a contemporary understanding of the Bible, and reason assists in making biblical selections for the lectionary. So the discoveries of natural science are recognized as a gift to Christian reception of the word. Thus, for example, the legend in Joshua 10 of the sun standing still so that the Israelites will win a battle is not appointed in the Revised Common Lectionary. A contemporary lectionary must decide when a twenty-first-century worldview influences the choice of Sunday's readings of a text two millenniums old.

Calendar Considerations

One example of "making all things new" that the Revised Common Lectionary shares with the Roman Catholic lectionary is the treatment of the Sunday of Holy Week. In the past, Palm Sunday was popularly dedicated to the proclamation of Jesus entering Jerusalem on the Sunday before his death. The distribution of palms made this occasion particularly festive. Worshipers heard the details of Jesus's arrest, trial, and execution only from the Gospel according to Matthew, and this reading of the passion was conducted at a time other than the primary service on that Sunday, with the Johannine passion proclaimed on Maundy Thursday and Good Friday. Which worshipers heard which biblical passages was determined in part by the lectionary, but also in part by patterns of worship attendance, which may not adhere to the logic of the lectionary.

The three-year lectionaries introduced a new way to keep Holy Week. The Sunday before Easter now has two focuses: Jesus's entry in Jerusalem and its palm procession functions as an introductory rite for the day, and then as the worship continues, the gospel reading is one or two chapters of the passion account, from Matthew in Year A, Mark in Year B, and Luke in Year C. In a masterful lectionary decision, these synoptic accounts that stress the sufferings of Christ are proclaimed on Sunday, which is always the day of Christ's resurrection. Then on Good Friday, the lectionary appoints the passion narrative from John, in which Jesus as God reigns from the cross. In what is an inspired juxtaposition, these triumphal accounts are proclaimed on the Friday of the commemoration of Jesus's death.

A calendar change that the Revised Common Lectionary inherited from the Common Lectionary was the introduction of a season of Epiphany. The Sundays that fall between Epiphany on January 6 and Ash Wednesday, which could fall anytime between February 7 and March 10, are designated as Sundays after the Epiphany and attend specifically to the beginning of Jesus's ministry. The readings feature especially in Year A the Sermon on the Mount, in Year B the healings that Jesus performed at the start of his ministry, and in Year C Jesus's preaching. The first Sunday after Epiphany is always kept as the baptism of Jesus. The last Sunday always celebrates the Transfiguration. On the Sunday of the

Transfiguration, the mountaintop revelation of Christ's glory contrasts the midweek Ash Wednesday and the journey of the whole Church together up the hill of Golgotha. Thus in the Revised Common Lectionary, the Sundays following after Epiphany have their own integrity, rather than being thought of as part of an "ordinary time."

Ecological Knowledge of the Cosmos

One area in which contemporary Christians question how to read and interpret the Bible concerns our ecological knowledge of the cosmos. The biblical descriptions of the earth are scientifically outdated, they would offend our reason were they presented as fact, and few biblical texts seem readily applicable for an ecological spirituality. Thus concerning ecology contemporary lectionaries experience a substantial gap between the biblical worldview and our knowledge and values.

The placement in the Revised Common Lectionary of the biblical passages that describe creation hope to make clear that the selections are not science lessons, but rather poetic texts that point the believer to God as the Creator and preserver of life. The first chapter of John is set for Christmas Day to praise the incarnate Christ as the Son of God from before creation. The opening chapter of Genesis is appointed for the Easter Vigil to present a parallel between the creation of the universe and the resurrection of Jesus Christ. The alternate creation story in Genesis 2:4b–14, in which God creates a garden as the source of the earth's four rivers, is not appointed in the lectionary.

Proverbs 8 is appointed for Trinity Sunday Year B, and suggests Wisdom as a picture of the Son of God active since the creation of the world. In the complementary readings from the Old Testament on Proper 7 Year B, Job's encounter with God in the whirlwind is set parallel with Jesus stilling the tempest. In the semicontinuous readings from the Old Testament on Proper 22 Year B, the passage from Job 28 occurs after Job 23 and before Job 42 to summarize the complex poetry of that book. Rather than describe scientifically how God formed the universe, the differences in details between Genesis 1 and Job 38 assist us in seeing both as rhetorically beautiful praises of the Creator.

One of the great gifts of the Revised Common Lectionary is its addition of the psalms to Sunday eucharistic worship. Many of the appointed psalms call believers to join with the whole of God's creation to praise the Creator, with the logical implication that we are to attend to the stewardship of the earth. Passages in the psalms that claim that the world "shall never be moved" (Ps. 93:1, 96:10) were used in the sixteenth century to support the notion that an unmovable earth was the center of the universe and thus to condemn Galileo for supporting heliocentrism. Yet in the lectionary, Psalm 93, appointed for Ascension Day, and Psalm 96, appointed for Christmas Eve, are set to music to praise the God who fills the cosmos and who was born into this earth. The seventeenth-century Lutheran astronomer Johannes Kepler suggested that, since sight is so central to human thought and action, the psalms were filled with language that described what people saw when they looked at the universe, rather than how scientists had come to understand the cosmos.[25] Contemporary Christians can once again delight in this way of seeing, this praise of the earth, the seas, and the skies by human eyesight, to call us into more ecological living. Singing the psalms helps us see the inexplicable splendor of creation, and many of these ancient poems offer texts that contrast with our selfish abuse and misuse of the earth.

That Christmas is celebrated near the winter solstice encourages Christians to attend to the movement of the earth around the sun and to praise God for such spectacular workings of the cosmos. That Easter is set in accord with the full moon and the spring equinox assists Christians to recognize also the things of the universe as indicative of God's renewal of life. Contemporary Christians can rediscover these most ancient occasions for communal worship on this earth, and so the readings and psalms of the Revised Common Lectionary become contemporary roadways in the journey toward more ecological living.

The readings appointed for Thanksgiving Day are ecologically significant passages, and users of the Revised Common Lectionary are thus encouraged to keep Thanksgiving as a harvest festival, rather than as a patriotic celebration. Alternatively, these readings could function in an annual festival of God's creation. In Year A, the first reading from Deuteronomy 8 includes a moving description

---

25. See Gail Ramshaw, "Reciting the Creed with Johannes Kepler," *Saints on Sunday: Voices from Our Past Enlivening Our Worship* (Collegeville, MN: Liturgical Press, 2018), 105–11.

of the bountiful earth God has provided, and Psalm 65 is one of the finest biblical poems praising the whole of God's creation. In Year B, the devastation brought about by a locust plague is contrasted with the fruitful fields that God provided, and the gospel reading is the treasured passage from the Sermon on the Mount about the birds and flowers of God's creation. In Year C, the passage from Deuteronomy 26 states that God has provided the harvest that feeds us, and Psalm 100 praises God who made us, to whom we belong.

The Role of Women

Chief among the decisions serving contemporaneity that were introduced by the framers of the Revised Common Lectionary is attention to women. In the first place, openness to the presence of women is served in part by the choice of which contemporary biblical translation is used in worship. Thus to prefer the cadence of the King James' Bible over the clarity of a recent American English translation diminishes the value of God's voice heard speaking to us in our time. An example of such translation issues is that, in rendering the Greek *adelphoi*, the translators of the NRSV have sometimes avoided "brothers," judging the male language as an inadequate way to address a mixed audience. An NRSV passage may read "brothers and sisters," "members of God's family," or a contextually appropriate noun such as "believers." But in the first place, the lectionary must do its best to represent biblical women and so incorporate them into the consciousness of the faithful. One example occurs at the Vigil of Easter. In the past, the story of the crossing of the Red Sea concluded with Moses leading the people in praise (Exod. 15:1). In the Revised Common Lectionary, Moses gives way to Miriam, as she leads the women in song and dance (Exod. 15:20–21).

Other women have entered the lectionary. On the fourth Sunday of Easter Year C, we hear the story of Dorcas, beloved for her works of charity. On the seventh Sunday of Easter Year C, we hear about the slave girl whose powers of divination profited her owners. On Proper 22 Year C, the grandmother Lois and mother Eunice are praised for having raised Timothy in the faith. Although it remains important for hearers to realize that "disciples" and "apostles" are categories that included women, every addition of a woman's name helps.

Central to the Revised Common Lectionary's commitment to the role of women has been a decision that is seldom seen, since it involves a deletion. Several places in the apostolic writings include or expand upon what are called the Household Codes (Eph. 5:22–6:9; Col. 3:18–4:1). In these standard first-century ethical injunctions, wives are to obey their husbands, and husbands are to care for their wives; children are to obey their parents, and fathers are to care for their children; slaves are to obey their masters, and masters are to treat their slaves honorably. In slave cultures, all three parts of the household codes remained important in Christian teaching. Since emancipation, the slave passage has been omitted in most Christian worship. It was left to the Revised Common Lectionary, when considering the passage that ordered the subjection of wives to their husbands, to delete the Household

Codes from the lectionary. Other New Testament passages that dictate women's conduct, dress, and subordinate social and religious role are not appointed in the Revised Common Lectionary. For example, the notorious verse that enjoins women to keep silent (1 Tim. 2:12) is not appointed in the Revised Common Lectionary.

The semicontinuous Old Testament selections for the time between the Sunday after Trinity and Reign of Christ include the stories of many women: in Year A, Sarah, Hagar, Rebekah, Leah, Rachel, the midwives, Pharaoh's daughter, and Deborah; in Year B, Michal, Bathsheba, Esther, Job's wife, Ruth, Naomi, Hannah, and the "capable wife" of Proverbs 31, who among other activities orders her serving women well; in Year C, the widow of Zarephath, Jezebel, Naaman's serving girl, and Gomer make their appearances. For those users of the Revised Common Lectionary who appoint these stories, it is important to remember that the details about these women were recorded centuries after their lifetimes, most likely by males. For those who use instead the complementary Old Testament readings, this listing provides a welcome agenda for Bible study outside of Sunday worship.

The Openness to Option

The contemporary Western world values option, not merely as a way to welcome personal choice, but as a postmodern sign that there is seldom one single absolute way forward. Thus in several places the Revised Common Lectionary offers options. That Christmas has multiple possible readings, that the Easter Vigil and

Easter Day list many possibilities, and that Pentecost offers a wide range to choose among are indications of the wealth of possible biblical passages for lectionary Christians to consider. That denominations or individual parishes can choose between two sets of Old Testament readings is perhaps the most consequential example of Revised Common Lectionary option. The lectionary provides three readings each Sunday for full eucharistic worship, but many Protestant worshiping communities choose to read only one or two of the selections.

Some preaching helps delineate a theme that means to govern the readings of each Sunday.[26] What is important for such a listing is the goal of each sermon. Such listings sometimes seem to suggest that the biblical readings are chosen to support a specific focus of the preaching. The Revised Common Lectionary does not provide any such arrow to which each set of readings aims. Rather, each lectionary set offers to the preacher, the musician, the artist, indeed, the entire assembly many options along which to travel.

An example can be seen in Proper 15 Year A. The gospel reading can be longer, including a teaching from Jesus about the origin of sin and evil, or it can be shorter, such as only the narrative of Jesus healing the daughter of a Canaanite woman. A careful preacher will notice that "Canaanite" is an anachronistic descriptor provided by Matthew to ground a xenophobic attitude in the distant past.

---

26. See, for example, Nils-Henrik Nilsson, "The Principles behind the New Sunday Lectionary for the Church of Sweden," *Studia Liturgica* 34 (Sept. 2004), 240–50.

In the first complementary reading from Isaiah 56, God promises to welcome "all peoples" into the life of the chosen community. In the semicontinuous reading from Genesis 45, Joseph forgives his brothers and welcomes them to Egypt. In the second reading, Paul affirms that God's covenant with the Jews is irrevocable. What of all these options might direct the primary emphasis for this Sunday? Some choices are: cultural prohibitions, human sinfulness, prejudice against the other, historic xenophobia, a disturbing anecdote about Jesus, praise for the woman's determination, and all this at the time of the opening of an academic year and the return of many worshipers to regular worship attendance. The lectionary does not stipulate a single thematic direction for worship, but rather narrows from hundreds to perhaps a dozen handles to hold on and pass around the mercy of God.

This chapter has hoped to illustrate some of the ways that the Revised Common Lectionary attends to today's real world. Which passages from the Bible should today's Sunday worshipers hear? Why? How do these selections fit with our understanding of scripture, our valuing of reason, our knowledge of the earth, our welcome of women, and our passion for justice? "Making all things new" is a tall order, and Revised Common Lectionary has tried its best to meet these challenges.

Questions for Reflection and Conversation

1. Choose a set of readings at random, and write a set of the Sunday intercessions that reflect those readings and attend to ecological concerns.

2. Do you wish that the Revised Common Lectionary included the Household Codes? Why or why not?

3. The semicontinuous Old Testament reading on Proper 7 Year B offers the unusual option of selecting either the narrative in 1 Samuel 17 of the fight between David and Goliath or the account in 1 Samuel 18 of the love between David and Jonathan. Which reading would you prefer, and why?

4. The Revised Common Lectionary newly introduced as a Gospel reading on Proper 10 Year B the unsettling account in Mark of the death of John the Baptist. What do you make of this addition? What might the preaching focus on?

5. A primary concern of contemporary Christians is the scourge of continuing prejudice against people of different skin color or ethnic origin. Locate among especially the second readings biblical passages that can apply to this concern.

6. When might some momentous local, national, or international event suggest that a parish replace the stipulated lectionary with other readings? Once a year? Never? Who would be authorized to make this choice?

6 ▪ There's Always More to Say About the Revised Common Lectionary

> For whatever was written in former days was written for our instruction, so that by steadfastness and by the encouragement of the scriptures we might have hope.
>
> Romans 15:4

In this concluding chapter, we will consider especially three features of the Revised Common Lectionary: that each lectionary set appoints three readings, that the Sunday readings have value all week long, and that the Revised Common Lectionary provides inspiration to artists and authors. The "much fine gold" that will serve us as illustrations are the readings for the first Sunday of Advent in Year A and for Proper 29, the last Sunday in Year C.

All Three Readings

In the past, it was common for Christian seminarians to be taught that either longer or shorter addresses, either sermons or homilies, were to focus on the gospel reading. Perhaps the logic was that since the Gospels dealt in a narrative fashion with the ministry of Jesus, and that since people like to listen to stories, the gospel reading provided the most welcome entry for the worshipers' attention. Many preachers understand their address as an imaginative elaboration on the gospel reading, enlarging upon the minimal details provided in the Bible with details that are profound, or clever, or in recent times humorous. Such attention solely on the gospel readings was a corrective to an earlier practice of delivering sermon series that might be topical or doctrinal, but often had no clear connection with whatever scripture had been proclaimed. However, to the extent that preachers seek to elaborate on the Gospels' narratives or to deliver one part of a thematic series, they may be unable to see the value in the Revised Common Lectionary's three readings.

Yet the lectionary seeks by means of the three readings to assist the preacher in staying on course. As Christians have stated since the early centuries of the Church, "Scripture interprets Scripture." In the Revised Common Lectionary, for at least half of each liturgical year, the first reading provides necessary background for the content of the gospel reading. Often the gospel reading directly interprets passages from the Old Testament. The first reading may even include a citation that is quoted in the gospel reading. On rare occasion, it offers a contrast that highlights the meaning of the gospel text.

The second reading, by attending to the life of the early Church, exemplifies the task of the preacher, for it establishes a link between the story of Jesus of Nazareth and the life of the body of Christ. A skilled preacher ought to be able to be helped by the first two readings to steer the gospel reading toward a communal hearing of the scriptures, the wealth of biblical passages supplying riches for the people, offering hope in the Spirit. Several denominational publishing houses are regularly issuing print and online commentaries, extraordinarily fine scriptural resources that assist our understanding of all the readings and any relationship among them. We can think of the three readings as similar to overlays in a biology textbook, in which each see-through sheet adds a deeper level from the interior to a study of what is outside.

To see an example of how the three readings interact, we can examine the readings for the first Sunday of the Revised Common Lectionary, the opening into Advent in Year A. The gospel reading is Matthew 24:36–44 and places in Jesus's mouth a prediction of the unexpected coming of the Son of Man. Here, the lectionary poses the liturgy several questions: what does Matthew mean by "the Son of Man"? Are the popular disaster films right, that all things are headed toward violent destruction? The first reading from Isaiah 2:1–5 assists our interpretation, by citing words from the prophet Isaiah in which God promises to bring renewal to the destroyed Jerusalem and peace to the whole world. What might be expected to be an approaching cataclysm, a second Noah's flood, a break-in by a thief, is corrected by the coming "light of the LORD." One might even say that on this first Sunday in Advent, the day's gospel, that is its good news, is in the first, rather than the third reading. It is helpful to recall that the Son of Man, that divine being who will vindicate the righteous and end the world's evils, is identified in the Christian Scriptures as Jesus himself.

Thanks to the second reading of Romans 13:1–14, we recall Paul's message that "the day" is near. In Christ is the beginning of that reordering of all things. In the Resurrection—remember, this is Sunday—we know that that chaos of human life can find salvation. We the baptized "put on" the Lord Jesus Christ now, and so are ready for "that day." For the day we anticipate is already here, and as the body of Christ, we are the arrival of the justice of God.

These readings begin Advent in Year A. The month of December in the Church is not meant to be consumed with holiday parties or pre-Christmas concerts. Rather, donning our baptismal robes, we are readying for Christ to appear, as indeed our Keeper is already recognized among us. We stand within the local, national, and international news, within what is personal and what is communal, and the three readings weave together to provide the sign of Christ that the lectionary superimposes on the fabric of the morning. The intention of the Revised Common Lectionary is that the three readings, far from being a biblical burden, are pointers to a full Christian meaning of the story of Jesus Christ that is proclaimed throughout the liturgy.

All Week Long

Many Christians maintain a daily discipline of scripture and prayer. The Book of Common Prayer provides one such listing for daily Bible selections in its Daily Office Lectionary. The readings are presented beginning with the Sundays and labeled in accord with the lectionary. Other lists of daily Bible readings are available, some with the intention of covering much of the Bible, others more focused on coordination with the liturgical year.

The Consultation on Common Texts released an impressive listing that corresponds directly with the Revised Common

Lectionary. Its list designates each Thursday through Saturday as Preparation for Sunday and each Monday through Wednesday as Reflection on Sunday.[27] For example, preparing for Proper 6 in Year B, on which the gospel reading is the parable of the mustard seed, the six readings include Genesis 3:14–24, as humans are deprived of the tree of life, and 2 Kings 14:1–14, in which the thornbush confronts a cedar of Lebanon. Then after Sunday, reflecting on the mustard seed parable, the six suggestions include Galatians 6:11–18, which proclaims that a new creation is everything, and Revelation 21:22–22:5, the description of the tree of life at the end of time.[28] By this means, the Sunday lectionary is expanded upon throughout the entire week.

Recently there has been a resurgence of interest in the sixth-century practice of *lectio divina*.[29] Designed by Benedict for a monastic community that dedicated four hours a day to the scripture, this practice allowed monks even while working in the fields to continue their attention to biblical passages. Foundational to the piety of Christians in England for a thousand years, *lectio divina* trains believers in attentive reading and devotional appropriation of the Bible. The discipline encourages personal reflections and open questions, and study is interspersed with prayer. When

---

27. Consultation on Common Texts, *Revised Common Lectionary Daily Readings* (Minneapolis: Fortress Press, 2005).
28. *Daily Readings*, 161.
29. See for example especially Jonathan Linman, "*Lectio Divina* and Holy Conversation," *Holy Conversation: Spirituality for Worship* (Minneapolis: Fortress Press, 2010), 31–49.

practiced in a group, *lectio divina* is egalitarian, respecting each contributor's comments. According to one pattern of use, the group or the individual reads a scriptural passage deliberately; after keeping a time of silence, reads it again to allow for deeper reception; after another time of silence, reads it again to inspire prayer; and after more silence, reads it yet again so as to absorb it into one's heart, mind, and behavior. There are various ways that participants might select the biblical passage or the single word that serve this discipline, but the lectionary offers itself for a weeklong practice of *lectio divina*.

Let us try *lectio divina* on Proper 29, the last Sunday of the liturgical year, the last Sunday after Pentecost in Year C. The gospel reading for the day, often called Reign of Christ or Christ the King, is Luke 23:33–43, a passage from the Lucan passion narrative with the uniquely Lucan emphasis on forgiveness, as Jesus forgives the soldiers and the repentant criminal. The crowd admits that Jesus has saved others. This is the setting—the crucified Jesus forgiving others—at which he is named "king of the Jews." From the cross he welcomes sinners into the royal garden of paradise. He is king where we least expect it: in the depth of our yearning for life, our suffering, and our need.

While we are gazing at the cross on Golgotha, the first reading from Jeremiah 23:1–6 shows us the ancient Near Eastern royal tree of life, the branch from King David that God will raise up to bring forth justice in the land. Christians see in Jeremiah's hope for righteousness this Jesus who is gathering into life all the scattered flock. The second reading, Colossians 1:11–20, is one of the New Testament's most magnificent creedal passages. To give Christian meaning to the story of the crucified Jesus, we praise Christ as the image of God, the Creator of the universe, the head of the body of the Church. Here at the close of the liturgical year we laud the sovereign Christ as the beginning of all things, from whom comes peace. Each line of the Colossian creed offers passages for our contemplation.

So what might *lectio divina* have to do with these readings? Similar to how the selected antiphon focuses our attention throughout an entire psalm, we can choose a sentence, phrase, or word from the Sunday readings to encapsulate the scripture of the day. The passage enters our mind, heart, and conduct, as day by day until the next Sunday we read, reread, ponder, pray, absorb, and resolve on its message. From Luke we might choose "Jesus, remember me." From Jeremiah we might choose "the LORD is our righteousness." We might sing each day Martin Luther's hymn on Psalm 46, "A mighty fortress is our God." From Colossians there are many possibilities: "the power of darkness," or "In Christ all things hold together," or "All the fullness of God was pleased to dwell in Christ." Our prayerful consideration of the text may be assisted by thoughts about our own biography, by knowledge of the needs of our neighbors and a suffering planet, by a silence underneath all words. Such a use of *lectio divina* makes the lectionary not only the guide that begins each week but also the companion of our Mondays through Saturdays.

So Many Authors and Artists

The adoption of the Revised Common Lectionary by many world-wide churches has encouraged the creative energies of many Christians. Recent collections of hymns and other assembly songs are filled with texts that refer explicitly or obliquely to lectionary choices. A sung text can successfully cite a relatively obscure biblical passage, which is known thanks to the presence of that passage in the lectionary, and a lectionary three times longer than the medieval lectionary provides familiarity with that much more Bible. New hymns are composed for lesser festivals that present the author's interpretation of the biblical narrative and thus serve as a complement to the interpretation offered by the preacher.

It is also in the visual arts that lectionary enthusiasm is apparent. Several websites offer lists of historic art that can be reproduced or projected to aid the assembly's reception of the texts.[30] It may be that the best use of screens that have been set up in the nave is for projection of each week's lectionary art. Whether the art is Rembrandt's moving depiction of the return of the prodigal son on the fourth Sunday of Lent in Year C or the Sunday school children's drawings of the six days of creation displayed during the Vigil of Easter, the lectionary has moved into visuals that assist our worship. Local artists provide their own work as part of the printed

---

30. One such site was compiled by David Stancliffe, the retired Bishop of Salisbury, England, *The Gospels in Art, Music, and Literature: The Story of Salvation in Three Media*, 3 vols (London: SPCK, 2013, 2014, 2015).

bulletin that serves the Sunday worship. Fabric art inspired by the lectionary is hung in the sanctuary. Art that coordinates with the week's texts adds visuals to worship without the controversial cost of erecting permanent art on the walls of the worship space.

The Revised Common Lectionary has gifted the Church around the globe with biblical readings that shine like gold in a darkened world. The Episcopal Church and worldwide Anglicans can rejoice in this liturgical jewel. The readings can stand by themselves: so, enter into them even before worship on Sunday. The readings enrich our biblical knowledge and open to us the avenues of salvation: so, treasure them during worship. The readings can inspire insightful preaching: so, hold out your hands to receive this gift. The readings can accompany you all week long: so, ponder one small glimmer of God's precious truth from Monday onward. The readings can inspire creative artistic offerings: so, welcome them into your journey of faith. As Paul said to the Christians in Rome, let what was written in former days encourage our life and give us hope.

Questions for Reflection and Conversation

1. How can the readings for the first Sunday of Advent stand against the society's December-long celebration of Christmas? Do you have any specific suggestions about this issue?

2. How can the imagery of the last Sunday of each year, that Christ reigns as king, function in a democracy? How is the image not merely anachronistic? Search online for images of the reigning Christ to see if any are liturgically profound in your setting.

3. Choose a set of readings at random, and see how the three readings interact with one another. How does the psalm complement the three?

4. Would the projection of visuals during worship assist the proclamation of the readings, or would it mostly be a distraction? Is it better that the visuals depict the Bible story or, rather, suggest a parallel from our lives?

5. Some assemblies offer midweek study sessions that examine the upcoming lectionary selections. Are there other useful suggestions to encourage the assembly to prepare beforehand for the Sunday proclamation, or is this an unrealistic hope of the "lectionary Christian"?

6. Which aspect of the Revised Common Lectionary most appeals to you, that it is ecumenical, metaphoric, historic, contemporary, or open to authors and artists? Which of these do you not care much about?

7. What has been the most surprising aspect of the Revised Common Lectionary that you have encountered during this study?

For Further Reading

Following are some significant lectionary resources that are not cited in the Endnotes:

Bower, Peter, ed. *Handbook for the Revised Common Lectionary*. Louisville: Westminster John Knox Press, 1996.

Consultation on Common Texts. *Revised Common Lectionary Prayers*. Minneapolis: Fortress Press, 2002.

Nocent, Adrien. *The Liturgical Year*. Three volumes. Trans. Matthew J. O'Connell. Introduced, Emended, and Annotated by Paul Turner. Collegeville, MN: Liturgical Press, 2013, 2014.

Ramshaw, Gail. *Treasures Old and New: Images in the Lectionary*. Minneapolis: Augsburg Fortress, 2002.

Ramshaw, Gail. *Word of God, Word of Life: Understanding the Three-Year Lectionaries*. Minneapolis: Augsburg Fortress, 2019.

West, Fritz. *Scripture and Memory: The Ecumenical Hermeneutic of the Three-Lectionaries*. Collegeville, MN: The Liturgical Press, 1997.

See also:

"Principles to Guide the Development of Liturgical Texts," Episcopal Church Task Force on Liturgical and Prayerbook Revision, October 2019.

Index of Primary Examples